THE TRIUMPH OF FRENCH PAINTING

Ingres to Matisse

THE TRIUMPH OF FRENCH PAINTING

Sona K. Johnston   William R. Johnston

The Baltimore Museum of Art
The Walters Art Gallery, Baltimore
in association with the Royal Academy of Arts, London

The exhibition is organized by
The Baltimore Museum of Art and the
Walters Art Gallery, Baltimore

First published in 2000 by
Scala Publishers Ltd
143–149 Great Portland Street
London W1N 5FB

Distributed outside the Walters Art Gallery,
The Baltimore Museum of Art and the
exhibition venues in the USA and Canada by
Antique Collectors' Club
Market Industrial Park
Wappingers Falls, New York 12590

ISBN (softcover edition)   1 85759 2557
ISBN (hardcover edition)   1 85759 259X

All measurements are in inches followed
by centimeters; height precedes width
precedes depth.

Printed and bound in Trieste, Italy
by Editoriale Lloyd s.r.l.

THE WALTERS ART GALLERY EDITOR
Deborah Horowitz
EDITOR   Moira Johnston
PHOTOGRAPHER FOR THE WALTERS ART GALLERY
Susan Tobin

ROYAL ACADEMY OF ARTS
The exhibition in London is sponsored by

BARCLAYS

The Royal Academy of Arts is grateful to Her
Majesty's Government for its help in agreeing
to indemnify the exhibition under the National
Heritage Act 1980, and to the Museums and
Galleries Commission for their help in
arranging this indemnity.

Plates I and II, on pages 34 and 37, illustrate
works which will be included in the exhibition
at the Royal Academy of Arts.

COVER/JACKET ILLUSTRATIONS
FRONT   Henri Matisse,
Purple Robe and Anemones, 1937, BMA 1950.261
BACK   Jean-Auguste-Dominique Ingres,
Oedipus and the Sphinx, 1864, 37.9
HALF-TITLE PAGE ILLUSTRATION
Pierre-Auguste Renoir,
Washerwomen, ca. 1888 (detail), BMA 1950.282
TITLE PAGE ILLUSTRATION
Jean-François Millet,
The Potato Harvest, 1855 (detail), 37.115

VENUES OF THE EXHIBITION
12 March–16 July 2000
The Baltimore Museum of Art
10 Art Museum Drive
Baltimore, Maryland 21218

13 August–26 November 2000
The Philbrook Museum of Art
2727 South Rockford Road
Tulsa, Oklahoma 74114

6 January–11 March 2001
Norton Museum of Art
1451 South Olive Avenue
West Palm Beach, Florida 33401

30 June–23 September 2001
Royal Academy of Arts
Burlington House
Piccadilly, London W1J 0BD

3 November 2001–6 January 2002
Albright-Knox Art Gallery
1285 Elmwood Avenue
Buffalo, New York 14222

CONTENTS

DIRECTORS' FOREWORD

Through the generosity of a number of its citizens, the city of Baltimore is fortunate to have two outstanding public art collections: The Baltimore Museum of Art and the Walters Art Gallery. At the BMA, the holdings represent the aggregate accomplishments of generations of charitable collectors, whereas those at the Walters were largely assembled by William T. Walters and his son, Henry, but have since been supplemented by other donors who built on that foundation.

Whether it was the senior Walters and George A. Lucas acquiring the paintings of their era, or the sisters Claribel and Etta Cone exploring the School of Paris, what unites these collectors was their singular commitment to the art of France. Fortunately, rather than duplicating each other's efforts, they created collections that have proved remarkably complementary.

Although both institutions maintain distinct identities, they have always remained united in their common goal of serving the community and have collaborated on numerous occasions in shared ventures. Now, we welcome this opportunity to draw upon our combined collections to present a broad overview of French painting from the early nineteenth century through the first decades of the twentieth century. In doing so, we honor both the acumen and generosity of Baltimoreans in the past. Finally, we would like to acknowledge the combined efforts of the staffs of the two museums in presenting *Ingres to Matisse: Masterpieces of French Painting*, especially its curators and authors, Sona and William Johnston. We would also like to express our gratitude to Sotheby's for its kind assistance with evaluating the works in the exhibition.

Doreen Bolger
DIRECTOR
THE BALTIMORE MUSEUM OF ART

Gary Vikan
DIRECTOR
THE WALTERS ART GALLERY

PRESIDENT'S FOREWORD

It is a great honour for the Royal Academy to be the sole European venue of this outstanding exhibition of works drawn from holdings of nineteenth- and early twentieth-century French paintings in the collections of The Baltimore Museum of Art and the Walters Art Gallery. Early in the nineteenth century, Baltimore overtook Boston as the third largest city in the United States, and was thus poised both to support the collecting of art and to encourage a sense of civic pride. Together these brought about the birth and fostered the continued growth of these two exceptional museums. Our relationship with them goes back a long time. Over the years, both have been generous lenders to our loan exhibitions, and in 1992/93 we organised the highly successful *Alfred Sisley* retrospective exhibition with the Walters Art Gallery. We are deeply indebted to their directors, Dr Doreen Bolger and Dr Gary Vikan, to their Trustees, and to their staff, notably Sona and William Johnston. We are also most grateful to Barclays who have generously agreed to sponsor the exhibition in London.

Professor Phillip King
PRESIDENT
ROYAL ACADEMY OF ARTS

SPONSOR'S FOREWORD

At Barclays we are committed to fostering enterprise and providing innovative financial solutions to our customers. This pioneering spirit reflects the attitude of the painters represented in the exhibition *Ingres to Matisse: Masterpieces of French Painting*. The exhibition traces the transition from the nineteenth to the twentieth century, a period when painting in France increasingly asserted its independence from officially endorsed art.

The extraordinary change in culture that came about in the mid-nineteenth century, triggered by the Industrial Revolution, is mirrored by the phenomenal IT revolution in today's society. The nineteenth century opened up access to art for many new sections of society, in the same way as the twenty-first century is opening up access for millions to information technology. The artists in this exhibition were pioneers in their creative responses to the changes going on around them. Barclays is also at the forefront of change, developing financial products and services for our customers.

In choosing an exhibition which celebrates a major period in the development of French painting, we are demonstrating our bond with Europe. We are delighted to sponsor *Ingres to Matisse: Masterpieces of French Painting* at the Royal Academy of Arts, the only venue in Europe to present this stunning exhibition.

We hope you enjoy the exhibition as much as we have enjoyed our association with it.

David Roberts
CHIEF EXECUTIVE, BUSINESS BANKING
BARCLAYS BANK PLC

The Baltimore Museum of Art
building in Wyman Park was
designed by John Russell Pope
in 1927 and opened in 1929
(BMA Archives)

THE BALTIMORE MUSEUM OF ART

Founded in 1914 by a dedicated group of civic leaders, The
Baltimore Museum of Art, with its collection of over 85,000
objects, ranging from ancient mosaics to contemporary works,
is Maryland's largest art museum. The Museum's renowned
Cone Collection, assembled by sisters Claribel and Etta Cone
in the first half of the twentieth century, is the cornerstone of
the permanent holdings and includes superb works by such
modern masters as Renoir, Cézanne, Van Gogh and Picasso,
in addition to a remarkably comprehensive assemblage of
paintings, sculpture, drawings and graphics by Henri Matisse.
Other notable areas of strength within the collection are
European Old Master paintings, American decorative arts and
paintings, art from Africa, Asia, the Americas and Oceania and
superb collections of prints, drawings and photographs.

   The Baltimore Museum of Art moved to its present Wyman
Park site in 1929, the year its main building, designed by John
Russell Pope, was completed.

William A. Delano's palazzo-
like building for the Walters Art
Gallery, which opened in 1909,
and its 1974 addition
(WAG Archives)

THE WALTERS ART GALLERY

In 1931, the City of Baltimore received one of its greatest
treasures when Henry Walters (1848–1931) bequeathed his art
gallery and his collection of 22,000 works of art to his native
city "for the benefit of the public." William T. Walters (1819–94),
Henry's father, had assembled a splendid collection of
nineteenth-century European art and Asian art, and under his
son's auspices the collection was transformed into one of the
finest American private collections. Henry Walters' interests
were boundless, ranging over 5,000 years, from ancient Egypt
to Art Nouveau. Although significantly expanded, the Museum's
strength and scope continue to reflect Mr Walters' collecting
acumen and philanthropic spirit. To meet the changing needs
of the Museum, a wing added in 1974 is presently undergoing
major renovations and will reopen in 2001.

THE COLLECTORS

At the beginning of the nineteenth century, Baltimore experienced phenomenal growth, bypassing Boston as the third largest city in the United States. Despite its new-found wealth as a major port, the city's cultural life was acknowledged by its citizens to be wanting. Elizabeth Patterson, the daughter of a prosperous resident, blamed the local men, whom she dismissed as "merchants lacking a single idea beyond their counting houses."[1] It was a complaint that would be echoed frequently throughout the nineteenth and early twentieth centuries. For Elizabeth, the solution was to find happiness through marriage to Jérome Bonaparte, the youngest brother of the future emperor of France. The dashing Jérome had arrived in Baltimore in the summer of 1803, and by the end of the year had succumbed to the charms of the comely 18-year-old. The union, however, proved ill-fated. Since Jérome lacked prior parental permission, the Emperor Napoleon annulled the marriage, but not before it gave rise to a Baltimore line of the Bonaparte family.[2]

Jérome Bonaparte did not initiate the city's ties to France, however. Both before and after his arrival there was a history of a French presence in Baltimore. Following their expulsion from Nova Scotia by the British in 1765, a number of Acadians, the original French settlers in North America, came to Baltimore. They were followed later in the century by royalist sympathizers from revolutionary France and by refugees fleeing uprisings on the Caribbean island of Hispaniola. The new arrivals tended to gravitate to a district known as Frenchtown. Among these immigrants were four members of the Sulpician religious order who reached the city in 1791 and converted an old tavern into St Mary's, a theological seminary originally intended to serve French-speaking refugees.

Constant Troyon
(French, 1810–65)
Coast near Villers, about 1859 (detail)
oil on canvas
The Walters Art Gallery, 37.993

Baltimore's links to France were reaffirmed when the Marquis de Lafayette made his triumphal return to America in 1824/5 (FIGURE 1). The Revolutionary War hero visited the city on several occasions, usually attending the theater or dining with former comrades-in-arms, but he also stopped at Peale's Museum and Gallery of The Fine Arts, founded by the painter Rembrandt Peale in 1814 as "an elegant rendezvous of taste, curiosity, and leisure."[3]

The political turmoil in France during the late eighteenth and early nineteenth centuries also prompted the visit to Baltimore of two Frenchmen of artistic bent who plied their respective trades and then moved on. Having arrived in New York in 1793, Charles Balthazar Julien Févret de Saint-Mémin, a painter and engraver from Dijon, spent considerable time in Baltimore between 1803 and 1807 producing delicate bust-length profile portrait drawings and watercolors of notable citizens, with the aid of a device called a physionotrace. After also working in Washington, Richmond and Charleston, South Carolina, Saint-Mémin returned to France in 1814 and served as director of the Musée des Beaux-Arts at Dijon until his death in 1852.

Fleeing from Napoleon's France, Maximilian Godefroy reached New York in April 1805, and by the end of the year was teaching drawing at St Mary's Seminary in Baltimore. In addition to designing the first Gothic Revival ecclesiastical building in America, the chapel at the seminary (completed in 1808), Godefroy's contributions to the city included two neoclassical structures, the Battle Monument, honoring those who died defending the city during the War of 1812, and the Unitarian Church (1817/18), which are considered to be his masterpieces. Prior to returning to his native Paris in 1827, Godefroy spent several years in London designing various buildings and exhibiting his drawings at the Royal Academy.

In the early 1820s, the first significant examples of current French painting reached Baltimore. These were presented to the Cathedral of the Assumption of the Blessed Virgin by Louis XVIII and his successor Charles X. In 1806, Archbishop John Carroll laid the cornerstone for the building, the first Roman Catholic cathedral in the United States. Prior to the consecration of the new sanctuary 15 years later, King Louis XVIII, at the request of Ambrose Maréchal, Baltimore's third archbishop, agreed to donate two large paintings to the new cathedral: Paulin-Jean-Baptiste Guérin's *Christ on the Knees of the Virgin Surrounded by Holy Women and Several Apostles* (for the church of Baltimore), which had been exhibited at the 1817 Paris Salon, and Baron Charles von Steuben's depiction of Louis IX, the revered saint

FIGURE 1 William Grimaldi
(English, 1751–1834)
*Portrait of the Marquis
de Lafayette*, after 1789
watercolor on ivory
The Walters Art Gallery, 38.109

and king, burying his troops at Tunis in 1270. These paintings still hang in the church, now reclassified as a basilica.

Although lacking many cultural amenities in the early nineteenth century, Baltimore claimed several notable art collectors. Like their counterparts in other American cities, these individuals both patronized regional artists and purchased Old Master paintings, which were often of dubious attribution. Among the earliest and most distinguished of these collectors was Robert Gilmor, Jr (1774–1848), the son of a Scottish immigrant who had established a successful mercantile house and amassed a sizable fortune (FIGURE 2). Educated abroad, Gilmor acquired a taste for art at an early age. As he predicted in 1797: "My fondness for the subject may prove dangerous, but as long as I can restrain it with[in] the bounds of prudence & reason, I am convinced it will prove one of the greatest sources of pleasure, amusement and relaxation from the serious concerns of life."[4]

In 1799, Gilmor embarked on a European Grand Tour that lasted over two years. The vast collection he ultimately assembled ranged over such diverse fields as classical artifacts, medieval manuscripts, Old Master paintings of Dutch, Flemish and Italian origin, drawings, prints, autographs and even mineral specimens. Gilmor also patronized contemporary American painters, in particular Thomas Doughty, Thomas Cole and William Sidney Mount, and the neoclassical sculptor Horatio Greenough. During a visit to London in 1818, Gilmor and his wife sat for Sir Thomas Lawrence, but there is scant evidence that they took any interest in contemporary French art. The collection did contain, however, a small group of seventeenth- and eighteenth-century French paintings that, for the most part, were by minor artists working in imitative styles.

Similarly, Thomas Edmondson (1808–56) studied medicine but preferred to lead the life of a dilettante, devoting himself to his artistic and horticultural interests. He collected copies of Old Master paintings as well as works by local artists, including Richard Caton Woodville, Alfred Jacob Miller and Ernst Fischer.[5] The largest art collection compiled in the city during the first half of the century was that of a merchant from England, Granville Sharp Oldfield (1794–1860). Consisting of 685 paintings, mostly spurious "Old Masters," a few minor American and English contemporary works and some prints, it was dispersed at auction in 1855.[6]

At mid-century, when Americans tentatively began to express their interest in contemporary European art, a few dealers specializing in the field opened galleries in New York. Michel Knoedler arrived from Paris in 1849 as representative of the firm

FIGURE 2 William James Hubard
(American, 1807–62)
Robert Gilmor, Jr, ca. 1830/2
oil on panel
The Baltimore Museum of Art
Charlotte G. Paul Bequest, BMA 1956.287

Goupil & Co. That year, John Böker opened the Dusseldorf Gallery in an abandoned church where he dealt in paintings by members of the Düsseldorf Kunstakademie. It was a challenging market, as the legendary Belgian dealer Ernest Gambart learned to his chagrin in 1857 when he failed to arouse any interest in a group of English paintings that he hoped to sell in New York, Philadelphia and Boston. He met with limited success two years later when he exhibited a number of French, Belgian and English paintings at the National Academy of Design in New York. The emergence of art publications also contributed to the growing awareness of foreign schools. Americans undoubtedly had access to copies of *The Art Journal*, a monthly chronicle devoted to the arts, which began publication in London in 1839. Likewise, in New York, *The Crayon* and *The Cosmopolitan Art Journal* appeared briefly in the late 1850s.

Baltimoreans, however, had unique access to the Paris art market through George A. Lucas (1824–1909). In the course of more than five decades during which he resided in the French capital, Lucas formed a remarkable collection of nearly 300 academic and Barbizon paintings, 18,000 prints and over 140 bronzes by Antoine-Louis Barye. In addition, he acted as agent for a small group of discerning collectors, including Samuel Putnam Avery and John Taylor Johnston of New York, and William and Henry Walters of Baltimore.[7]

One of eleven children of Fielding Lucas, Jr, a Baltimore bookseller and publisher, and his wife, Eliza M. Carrell, young George abandoned a career as a civil engineer to settle in Paris, where he remained from 1857 until his death. He meticulously recorded in his diaries all his activities, ranging from the most mundane aspects of his daily routine to his many visits to artists' studios. While the diaries offer little insight into any personal relationships that Lucas may have developed during the course of these encounters, they provide a comprehensive overview of his passionate involvement in the Paris art world throughout the second half of the nineteenth century.

Among Lucas's early acquaintances in Paris was James A. McNeill Whistler, a fellow graduate of West Point. Although Lucas would acquire most of Whistler's etchings, he never purchased a painting. Whistler remarked in 1862, when his friend briefly contemplated such an addition to his holdings: "I'll be charmed to find myself in your collection which, I thought, you never would have shocked with one of my productions."[8]

If Lucas confined his enthusiasm for Whistler's art to prints, his admiration for the work of the *animalier* Antoine-Louis Barye was all encompassing. The collector first visited Barye's studio

Jean-Baptiste-Camille Corot
(French, 1796–1875)
Sèvres-Brimborion, View towards Paris, 1858/64 (detail)
oil on canvas
The Baltimore Museum of Art
George A. Lucas Collection,
BMA 1996.45.66

on 26 December 1859, and he would acquire not only sculpture, but paintings, watercolors, drawings and prints as well. Lucas also introduced the sculptor to a number of clients who would collect his work.

For the most part, the paintings in the Lucas collection are modest in scale. While many are finished works, others appear to be sketches, and a number bear dedications to the collector, possibly gifts from artists in gratitude for commissions. Most importantly, the collection, while reflecting Lucas's tastes in an intimate and personal manner, also presents an insight into the artistic trends and concerns manifest in Paris during the period. Works by academic painters such as Gérôme and Bouguereau speak to more traditional tastes, but Lucas also recognized the significance of more progressive artists, including Daumier, Couture and the Barbizon masters. In particular, Corot's *Sèvres-Brimborion, View towards Paris*, 1858/64 (no. 8), anticipates the impressionists' paintings of the 1870s. Similarly, Pissarro's *Path by the River* (no. 29), painted in 1864, foreshadows the artist's espousal of the movement as manifest in his winter landscape from ca. 1869, *Route to Versailles, Louveciennes* (no. 30).

Indicative of George Lucas's expansive interests is his collection of more than 70 artists' palettes, many, like some of his paintings, bearing dedicatory inscriptions and sketches. On the reverse, the collector often made notations and attached clippings of pertinent information, a practice that he also followed with his paintings.

A description provided by Whistler biographer Elizabeth R. Pennell, after her visit in February 1904 to Lucas's apartment on the rue de l'Arc de Triomphe, offers a sympathetic account of the elderly collector:

> He was then eighty—like a prophet with his white beard, and in his long gray flannel coat and gray scull cap, sitting in a fairly small room, delightfully littered with his collections; the walls hung as close as possible with pictures—two Corots, a Daumier, a Hervier and more than I had time to look at against the walls, two or three little cabinets covered with small bronzes by Barye, and a few low cases filled with portfolios labeled *Whistler, Manet, Jacque* [FIGURE 3].[9]

Toward the end of his life, George Lucas became increasingly concerned about the ultimate fate of the collection. According to a nephew, William F. Lucas, Jr, it had long been his desire to find a home for his holdings in his native city. In consultation with his friend Henry Walters, whom he had known since the latter's first visit as a boy to Paris with his family in the 1860s, Lucas

FIGURE 3 Dornac, *George A. Lucas*, 1904
photograph
(WAG Archives)

chose as his beneficiary the Maryland Institute, an art school of which his father, Fielding Lucas, Jr, had been a founder in 1826. Following Lucas's death in December 1909, Walters arranged for the transport of the collection from Paris to Baltimore.[10]

William Thompson Walters (1819–94) was not only among the first Baltimoreans to collect contemporary art, but he also played a significant role in establishing its popularity elsewhere in the country (FIGURE 4).[11] A native of central Pennsylvania, Walters was drawn to the city in 1840, attracted by its burgeoning economy. Upon his arrival he joined a "commission merchant" house dealing in grain and flour, but within a decade he struck out on his own, establishing William T. Walters and Company, a wholesale liquor firm that distributed rye whiskey and other beverages to a wide market, particularly in the South. He soon prospered and in 1857 he moved with his wife, Ellen, and two children, Henry and Jennie, to a handsome residence on Mount Vernon Place, a fashionable district on an elevation overlooking downtown (FIGURE 5).

William Walters credited his mother for his early taste for art and recalled how she had once offered him the following advice:

> The busy portions of a young man's life . . . are taken
> up full enough to keep him out of mischief or
> contamination. It is his leisure time and surplus money
> that must be provided for and a young man can employ
> his time appreciating in no better way than by devoting
> them to accumulating and appreciating the noble works
> of literature and art.[12]

Like many of his contemporaries, Walters patronized local talent and also delved into the New York art market, commissioning works from Asher B. Durand, John Frederick Kensett and other members of the Hudson River School of landscape painting.

In an audacious move, Walters purchased Jean-Léon Gérôme's *The Duel after the Masquerade*, painted in 1857/8 (no. 22), for $2,500 from the Belgian dealer Ernest Gambart's 1859 exhibition at the National Academy of Design. A replica of the artist's *Suite d'un bal masqué* (1857), *The Duel after the Masquerade*, had generated considerable interest when it was exhibited in London the previous year. At the same time, Walters also obtained nine other French and Belgian genre paintings. Later that year, Walters commissioned his first work from abroad. With George Lucas acting as intermediary, he ordered a picture from Hugues Merle, an academic figurative painter whose reputation was then ascendant at the Paris salons. Walters requested a quintessentially American subject, Hester Prynne

FIGURE 4 Bendann,
William T. Walters, ca. 1870s
photograph
(WAG Archives)

and her illegitimate daughter, Pearl, as described in Nathaniel Hawthorne's novel *The Scarlet Letter*, published in 1850.

At the outbreak of the Civil War, William Walters, who had long championed "states' rights" and had benefited from extensive commercial ties with the South, decided that it was an opportune moment to take his family abroad. Upon their arrival in Paris in August 1861, they were greeted by George Lucas, who introduced them to the city's museums and guided them to artists' studios and to dealers, often serving as agent whenever they decided to make a purchase. Particularly fortuitous was an encounter with Antoine-Louis Barye in September of that year. The artist had begun to receive official recognition after years of neglect, and it was Walters, assisted by Lucas, more than any other patron, who would subsequently assure his reputation in America.

While abroad, William and Ellen undertook a number of excursions, visiting Italy and Switzerland in the spring of 1862. That autumn they attended the International Exhibition in London where William was captivated by a display of Japanese and Chinese artworks, especially ceramics, which would eventually become a life-long obsession rivaling his commitment to European art. Their visit to England ended tragically when Ellen succumbed to pneumonia, leaving William with the two children to rear.

Perhaps as a source of solace, Walters immersed himself in the art market. During a visit to Corot's studio in 1864, he saw *L'Étoile du berger* (Toulouse, Musée des Augustins) in progress

FIGURE 5 E. Sachse & Co.,
View of Baltimore City, MD., 1872
lithograph
The George Washington Monument (1815/29), designed by Robert Mills, stands in the center of the four arms of Mount Vernon Place. William T. Walters' residence is the third house to the right of the Monument. Continuing in the same direction, the house at the southwest corner intersection was built for John Work Garrett and, in 1916, became the temporary home of The Baltimore Museum of Art. Looking south toward the harbor, just to the right of the Monument, are two domed structures, the nearest being Maximilian Godefroy's First Unitarian Church (1818) and the second the Basilica of the Assumption, designed by Benjamin H. Latrobe with later additions.
(Courtesy of the Maryland Historical Society)

but declined to pay the artist's asking price, preferring instead to commission a smaller replica, *The Evening Star*, 1864 (no. 9). That year the resourceful Walters entered into a business arrangement with New York art entrepreneur Samuel Putnam Avery. Walters would provide the capital, and George Lucas the expertise, to enable Avery to launch himself as a dealer in New York. How long this agreement remained in effect is not documented, but as a result of the alliance Avery emerged as one of the country's most influential champions of European art.

On 7 March 1865, 33 days before General Robert E. Lee's surrender at Appomattox, Walters, sensing the Civil War was about to end, left Paris with his family for home. Back in Baltimore, he abandoned the liquor business and, together with several other local financiers, began to invest in the Carolina railroads, which had been devastated by the war. Eventually, these and a number of other lines would be consolidated to create the Atlantic Coast Line Railroad, serving the southeastern United States.

Walters now found himself in the vanguard of American collectors who played a dominant role in the Paris art trade during the second half of the century. Periodically, he returned to Europe, taking pride in attending the principal international exhibitions, especially when he was designated honorary United States commissioner to the 1873 Vienna international exhibition. With

FIGURE 6 An exhibition of nineteenth-century art at The Baltimore Museum of Art during World War II. At the extreme right is J. L. Gérôme's *Dead Caesar*, lent by the Corcoran Gallery of Art. A print of J. A. D. Ingres' *Oedipus and the Sphinx* has been substituted for the original painting, which was stored in a bomb-proof shelter. (BMA Archives)

Lucas as his representative, he continued to order works abroad, acquiring from Charles Gleyre, in 1867, a replica of the celebrated *Le Soir* from 1843 (no. 21), which the Swiss artist claimed recorded a vision he had experienced one evening on the banks of the Nile River. Walters' other source for European paintings was the New York market. He followed the auctions at Chickering Hall, successfully bidding for pictures at sales of the collections formed by William T. Blodgett and John Taylor Johnston (both in 1876), John Wolfe (1882), Mrs Mary Jane Morgan (1886) and Henry Probasco (1887).

In 1869, William W. Corcoran deeded his gallery and collection to the public, establishing Washington, D.C.'s first institution devoted to art. Recognizing Walters' expertise, Corcoran invited him to serve as one of nine trustees of the Corcoran Gallery of Art. In addition, he designated the Baltimorean as chairman of the Committee on Works of Art. Under Walters' leadership, the Corcoran purchased a number of major salon paintings, including Gérôme's masterly example of foreshortening, *Dead Caesar*, 1857 (FIGURE 6).[13]

Walters' experiences at the Corcoran Gallery undoubtedly determined the course of his own collecting. A seriousness of purpose began to replace the seemingly random nature of his earlier buying. Outstanding later additions include Jean-François Millet's *The Sheepfold, Moonlight*, acquired before 1879 (no. 17), Théodore Rousseau's *Effet de Givre*, acquired 1882 (no. 13), Corot's monumental *Saint Sebastian Succored by Holy Women*, acquired 1883, and Eugène Delacroix's *Christ on the Cross*, acquired 1886 (no. 5). An ardent proselytizer for art, Walters welcomed visitors to his Mount Vernon Place home. In the spring of 1874 he opened his residence to the public, charging a 50-cent admission fee and donating the proceeds to the Baltimore Association for the Improvement in the Condition of the Poor. He repeated this event in 1876, and, beginning in 1878, he made it an annual occurrence, which was eagerly anticipated by Baltimoreans each spring. By 1883 the collection had outgrown the house. Acquiring a property to the rear, Walters bridged an alley and converted an adjoining stable into a sky-lighted picture gallery, which he opened the following winter (FIGURE 7).

In a similar spirit, William Walters issued a series of catalogues of his paintings. The first, which appeared in around 1878, was somewhat of an amateur production, merely naming works and including an occasional remark. Subsequent catalogues, however, beginning in 1884, listed artists' dates, their teachers and various awards they had received, and also reproduced excerpts from their letters. The most ambitious publication was *Notes*

Critical and Biographical; Collection of W. T. Walters (1895), which contained a text of "word paintings" written by the Indianapolis artist Richard B. Gruelle describing the individual works.

Many Baltimoreans must have hoped that Walters would follow precedents set by the philanthropists George Peabody, Johns Hopkins and Enoch Pratt and provide for a public institution.[14] Instead, when he died in 1894, William bequeathed the art collection to his son, Henry.

Although William T. Walters unquestionably dominated the Baltimore art scene in the post Civil War era, there were other collections in town, but critics remained sharply divided as to their significance. John R. Tait, writing for *Lippincott's Magazine* in 1883, observed: "It is hard to determine which of the two facts is more surprising—that Baltimore should have produced so many excellent artists, or, that she should have remained so indifferent to art." He continued: "in bright contrast with this indifference of the many is the intelligent love of the few," and cited as examples Robert Gilmor, Jr, and J. Stricker Jenkins, Jr, both long dead, John Work Garrett, president of the Baltimore and Ohio Railroad, and Walters.[15] Several years earlier, on the other hand, Earl Shinn, in surveying the nation's private collections, commented of Baltimore:

> There are several parlor collections of great interest among the splendid homes of this ancient and beautiful city, where the warm enthusiasm of the South finds itself hospitable to every form and development of art, in distinction from the dilettante clannishness of the North too prone to make fetishes of its Millets and Corots.[16]

With several exceptions, these other collections to which Shinn alluded were mostly situated in the vicinity of Mount Vernon Place and contained American works interspersed with a smattering of paintings by either French artists or those of other nationalities who exhibited in Paris. For example, a merchant, David T. Buzby, owned several noteworthy paintings by Alexandre Cabanel and William Bouguereau. John Work Garrett added a picture gallery to his house at the west end of Mount Vernon Place to display his European and American works. His French holdings included paintings by Georges Clairin, Jean-Léon Gérôme, one of Félix Ziem's ubiquitous views of the Grand Canal in Venice and a number of small genre paintings by the *petits maîtres* Théophile Duverger, Jean-Baptiste Fauvelet and Charles Zacharie Landelle.

Had he visited the city before 1876, Shinn would undoubtedly have reviewed the collection of Col. J. Stricker Jenkins (1831–78), one of the six founders of Maryland's Fifth Regiment. The son

FIGURE 7 William T. Walters'
gallery behind his Mount
Vernon Place residence, 1884
photograph
(WAG Archives)

of an Irish immigrant who had established a business in the city importing coffee from Brazil, Jenkins began to collect in the mid-1850s. His tastes were eclectic, and by 1870, the year in which he published a catalogue of his holdings, he had acquired 47 American and 45 European paintings.[17] Many of the French works were by once popular artists whose reputations have since declined. In this category were Emile Beranger, Léon Caille, François Compte-Calix, Antoine Emile Plassan and Paul Signac. A highlight of the collection was Bouguereau's *Art and Literature*, 1867, a large composition with idealized, life-size figures representing the two muses (New York, Elmira, Arnot Museum). With George Lucas as his intermediary, Jenkins commissioned this work in 1866, and it became the first of the artist's paintings to come to America. In 1875, Edward King, in *Scribner's Magazine*, predicted that the Walters and Jenkins collections would one day be combined to form the nucleus of a public museum of which the city could "justly be proud."[18] It was not to be; a year later, Jenkins sold his paintings at auction in New York. He died in 1878, at the age of only 47.

During America's late nineteenth-century "Gilded Age," social and economic changes gave rise to vast fortunes and, inevitably, to major shifts in taste. The new Maecenases, whose Beaux-Arts styled mansions lined New York's Fifth Avenue and dotted other cities, tended to be better traveled and more sophisticated than preceding generations. In art collecting, they turned from salon paintings, formerly so avidly sought, to the Old Masters, French eighteenth-century art and to English society portraits, thereby establishing a subtle link with the princely collectors of the past. To assist them were a number of dealers both abroad and in the United States, including, in New York, Joseph Duveen, Knoedler & Company and Joseph Seligmann, among others.

In Baltimore, Mary Sloan Frick (1851–1936) followed this shift in taste (FIGURE 8). After her marriage in 1872 to Robert Garrett, who would succeed his father, John Work Garrett, as president of the Baltimore and Ohio Railroad, she established her reputation as the doyenne of Baltimore society and one of the most influential women in local philanthropic and cultural matters. The couple's townhouse on Mount Vernon Place was in a constant state of renovation. With additions by Stanford White and John Russell Pope, it emerged as a 40-room brownstone mansion more closely resembling the New York architecture of the period than the classical-revival houses on the square. When the Garretts began to collect is not documented, but, in 1887, a French visitor, Edmond Durand-Gréville, noted portraits by Elizabeth Vigée-Lebrun, Jean-Marc Nattier and François-Hubert Drouais in their parlor. In 1896, Robert Garrett died after a lingering illness, and six years later, Mary married his private physician, Henry Barton Jacobs. She continued to augment the collection, acquiring such paintings as Rembrandt's portrait of his son Titus, a Frans Hals, portraits by Raeburn, Romney and Hoppner and a number of exceptional works by the French eighteenth-century masters Quentin de la Tour, Hubert Robert, Fragonard and Greuze. She had only one significant nineteenth-century painting, her own portrait at the age of 34, executed by Alexandre Cabanel. A powerful image, it conveys the personality of the subject, whose greatest delights were "her home, her church, her flowers and her carriage."[19] In 1934, two years before her death, Mary Frick Jacobs promised the collection to The Baltimore Museum of Art with the proviso that a gallery be built

FIGURE 8 Alexandre Cabanel
(French, 1823–88)
Portrait of Mary Frick Garrett (later Mrs Henry Barton Jacobs), 1885
oil on canvas
The Baltimore Museum of Art
Mary Frick Jacobs Collection,
BMA 1938.238

in which to display it. The Museum, founded in 1914, had moved into a new building designed by John Russell Pope at its present Wyman Park site in 1929.

Among Baltimore's other civic-minded individuals during the first half of the twentieth century was Jacob Epstein (1864–1945) who came to the United States as a young man from Lithuania (FIGURE 9).[20] He arrived in the city in 1879 and opened a notions shop, which eventually became the "Baltimore Bargain House." The company prospered and by 1919, when it was re-named the "American Wholesale Corporation," it had become a $45 million-a-year business. Epstein retired in 1929 and devoted his remaining years to charities, travel and his art collection. He was a firm believer in giving as the need arose and generously supported a wide range of causes. He was on such cordial terms with Baltimore's Cardinal Gibbons that mutual friends jocularly alluded to the pair as the prince of priests and the prince of trade.[21]

Like many collectors during the 1880s and 1890s, Epstein initially focused on nineteenth-century paintings. Among his early purchases were works by such popular artists as Alphonse De Neuville, a specialist in military subjects, Jean-Charles Cazin and Camille Corot, two painters whose tranquil, atmospheric landscapes were particularly desirable at this time (no. 12). He favored paintings by the artists who specialized in rural subjects and were associated with the village of Barbizon on the edge of the Fontainebleau Forest, but was also attracted to works by members of The Hague School, including Hendrick Mesdag, Anton Mauve and Joseph Israels. In sculpture, he limited himself to a few significant bronzes by Antoine-Louis Barye and Auguste Rodin. During the 1920s, Epstein disposed of many of his earlier acquisitions and turned to the Old Masters. Among his most exceptional purchases were Anthony van Dyck's early master-piece *Rinaldo and Armida*, painted for Charles I of England, and Raphael's *Portrait of Emilia Pia de Montefeltro*, both acquired in the 1920s. In 1908, Jacob and his wife, Lena, moved to a large house on fashionable Eutaw Place, where he displayed his nineteenth-century paintings in a white and gold drawing room, and allocated works from earlier schools to a large "Moorish Room" lined in dark red fabric. One of the founding trustees of The Baltimore Museum of Art, Epstein placed his collection on loan in 1929 for the opening of the present building. With his death in 1945, it was bequeathed to the Museum, dramatically expanding the Old Master holdings.

Abram Eisenberg (1860–1933), a close acquaintance of Epstein, shared an enthusiasm for collecting. At the age of six he arrived in the United States from Hungary and grew up

FIGURE 9 Sir William Orpen
(British, 1878–1931)
Jacob Epstein, 1927
oil on canvas
The Baltimore Museum of Art,
BMA 1951.113

in Lonaconing in western Maryland. He always maintained that he had first manifested an interest in art when he paid the "exorbitant" admission price of 50 cents to view Jean-François Millet's *The Angelus* when it was displayed, perhaps surprisingly, in Cumberland, Maryland. A long-forgotten episode in the history of the painting is the fact that it was sent on an American tour during the fall and winter of 1889 after it was sold that year in the controversial and much publicized E. Secrétan sale.[22]

Eisenberg moved to Baltimore as a young man and opened a retail business. Like Epstein, Eisenberg was attracted to the Barbizon school and bought landscapes by Diaz, Daubigny (no. 19) and Troyon, but, unlike his friend, he ignored the Old Masters and instead, with his wife, Helen, he became one of the first Baltimoreans to delve into the market for impressionist work. Among the collection's works were Renoir's appealing portrait of a child holding a hoop (no. 38) and two London views by Claude Monet, *Charing Cross Bridge ("Reflections on the Thames")*, 1901/4, and *Waterloo Bridge ("Effect of Sun and Smoke")*, 1903 (nos. 34 and 35). Eisenberg died in 1933, but his widow continued to add to the collection, acquiring Corot's *Crown of Flowers*, ca. 1865/70 (no. 11), and examples of English portraiture.

Henry Walters stands apart from other Baltimore collectors at the beginning of the twentieth century in the scope of his interests and the zeal with which he pursued his objectives (FIGURE 10).[23] Ironically, he was a Baltimorean only *in absentia*. After the family's return from France at the close of the Civil War, he was enrolled at Georgetown College in Georgetown (now Washington), D.C., and subsequently pursued studies in engineering at Lawrence Scientific School in Cambridge, Massachusetts. His first employment was with the Pittsburgh and Connellsville Railroad, a subsidiary of the Baltimore and Ohio Railroad operating in Virginia, and later he joined the Atlantic Coast Line at its headquarters in Wilmington, North Carolina. By 1894, the year of his father's death, he had risen to the position of general manager.

In the late 1890s, the railroad moved its headquarters to New York City. Henry Walters led a peripatetic existence, staying in New York with his close friends from Wilmington, the Pembroke Joneses, or visiting them in their residences in North Carolina and Newport, Rhode Island. He listed his summer addresses in the Social Register as either abroad or on his steam-yacht, the *Narada*.

Henry was 46 when he inherited his father's art collection. His bonds with his widowed father had remained particularly close, and he had frequently participated in the acquisition of

Jean-Baptiste-Camille Corot
(French, 1796–1875)
The Crown of Flowers, 1865/70 (detail)
oil on canvas
The Baltimore Museum of Art
The Helen and Abram Eisenberg
Collection, BMA 1968.36

works, especially in the fields of Japanese and Chinese art. His aspirations as a collector, however, would far surpass those of the senior Walters. An extremely reticent man, he never disclosed his goals, but in hindsight it would appear that from the outset he intended to create a comprehensive collection that would provide the basis for a public museum in the city of his birth. Many years of service as an active trustee at The Metropolitan Museum of Art in New York undoubtedly helped to prepare him for this pursuit. Together with Mrs Henry Barton Jacobs, he was also appointed one of the Incorporators of The Baltimore Museum of Art.

There were early indications of his ambitious intentions. In June 1900, he bought Raphael's *Madonna della Candelabra*, the first example of the artist's then most coveted subject to enter the United States. That September, Henry acquired three houses on Charles Street in Mount Vernon adjoining the property his father had used for his 1884 gallery. Two years later, in a purchase then unprecedented in the annals of American collecting, he acquired the contents of the Palazzo Accoramboni in Rome. It contained over 1,700 objects, among them Roman and Etruscan antiquities, early Italian paintings and Renaissance and Baroque works of art, all of which had been assembled during the second half of the nineteenth century by Don Marcello Massarenti, a priest and fiduciary agent at the Vatican. The construction of a gallery in Baltimore to house the collection could no longer be postponed. During a visit to Venice in 1903, Henry Walters encountered William A. Delano, who only recently had received his diploma at the École des Beaux-Arts in Paris. He engaged the young architect to design the palazzo-like structure for the Charles Street site, which was ready to receive visitors early in 1909.

Although it would represent a minor facet of his collecting, Henry Walters continued to augment the holdings of nineteenth-century French painting acquired by his father. With the benefit of historical perspective, he endeavored to broaden the collection to include significant works that generally either pre-dated or post-dated his father's acquisitions. In 1899, he purchased Eugène Delacroix's freely rendered *Sketch for the Battle of Poitiers*, 1829/30 (no. 4), and in 1900 he bought his first painting by Jean-Auguste-Dominique Ingres, *The Betrothal of Raphael and the Niece of Cardinal Bibbiena*, 1813/14 (no. 2). Five years later, he added a more monumental work by the master, *Oedipus and the Sphinx*, 1864 (no. 3), which represented the elderly artist's return to a subject he had first explored in 1808 while a student at the Villa Medici in Rome.

FIGURE 10 *Henry Walters*, ca. 1907
photograph
(WAG Archives)

Jean-Auguste-Dominique Ingres
(French 1780–1867)
*The Betrothal of Raphael and the
Niece of Cardinal Bibbiena*, 1813/14
oil on paper mounted on canvas
The Walters Art Gallery, 37.13

Although he had ample opportunity to become familiar with the French impressionists, Henry, like his father, tended to shun them, preferring instead pictures that were "well finished." Perhaps moved by an obligation to be more comprehensive in his tastes, he purchased in 1900 Alfred Sisley's sweeping view of the Seine Valley, *The Terrace at Saint-Germain, Spring*, 1875 (no. 36), when the artist was painting in his fully developed impressionist manner. In 1902, Walters accompanied George Lucas to Mary Cassatt's Paris apartment, where he was persuaded to buy Claude Monet's *Springtime*, ca. 1872, a small painting representing the artist's wife, Camille, seated under a lilac bush, as well as Edgar Degas' *Portrait of Estelle Musson*, 1863/5. He added another Sisley to the collection in 1909, *View of Saint-Mammès*, 1881 (no. 37), but it was in the following year that he made perhaps his most daring purchase, Edouard Manet's *The Café-Concert*, 1878/9 (no. 28), which shows figures seated at the bar of the Café de Reichshoffen, painted toward the end of the artist's life. Upon their arrival in Baltimore, however, all of these paintings, with the exception of the early Sisley and the Monet, were consigned to storage in the basement.

Henry demonstrated how thoroughly he had been imbued with a taste for academic art in his youth at an auction held in New York in 1917. On that occasion, four years after the Armory Show had presented Cubism to American viewers, he successfully placed bids for four paintings by Jean-Léon Gérôme, including *The Death of Caesar*, 1867 (no. 23), which he recalled having seen in the artist's studio 50 years earlier. Ironically, when the Walters Art Gallery opened as a public institution in 1934, three years after Henry's death, visitors and critics alike, perhaps overcome by the density of the holdings in other areas, still gravitated to the galleries with the nineteenth-century paintings.

In many respects, The Cone Collection formed by Claribel (1864–1929) and Etta Cone (1870–1949) during the first half of the twentieth century is synonymous with The Baltimore Museum of Art.[24] Raised in Victorian Baltimore, the sisters amassed a wide-ranging collection that included not only French painting, sculpture and graphic art from the nineteenth and early twentieth centuries, but also Near Eastern and European textiles and decorative arts, jewelry, Japanese prints and a small number of antiquities. It was their shared passion for the art of Henri Matisse, however, that led to the formation of one of the most comprehensive assemblages of his work anywhere. These holdings eventually included 42 paintings, 18 sculptures, 36 drawings, 155 prints and 7 illustrated books. The paintings range in date from 1896 to 1947, with the greatest concentration in the 1920s

Jean-Léon Gérôme
(French 1824–1904)
A Roman Slave Market, ca. 1884
oil on canvas
The Walters Art Gallery, 37.885

FIGURE 11 *Gertrude Stein,
Etta and Claribel Cone,
Vallombrosa, Summer,* 1903
photograph
(The Baltimore Museum
of Art, Cone Archives)

and 1930s. Although Claribel Cone is generally credited with making the more adventurous purchases, the sisters' Matisse holdings, as well as their superb collection of works by Picasso, reflect a somewhat conservative taste, not unlike the preferences of earlier collectors, such as George Lucas and William and Henry Walters in their eras. Nevertheless, the Cones, like their predecessors, were drawn to the art of their time and left an extraordinary and rich legacy to the citizenry of Baltimore.

Claribel and Etta, daughters of Herman Cone and his wife, Helen Guggenheimer, grew up in Baltimore in a large family of a dozen children. While Etta's formal education ended with her graduation from high school in 1887, Claribel, six years her senior, pursued medical studies in Baltimore and Philadelphia, specializing in pathology. With the death of their father in 1897, the young women shared an inheritance with their siblings that assured an ample, if not luxurious, existence.

In 1898, charged with the management of the family household, Etta, in an attempt to enliven the living quarters, purchased five paintings by the American impressionist Theodore Robinson at his New York estate sale. These works, which undoubtedly startled Baltimoreans with their bright color and vigorous brushwork, were the first impressionist canvases to enter the city and became the nucleus of The Cone Collection.

FIGURE 12 Pablo Picasso
(Spanish, 1881–1973)
Bonjour Mlle Cone
pen and ink
The Baltimore Museum of Art
The Cone Collection, formed by
Dr Claribel and Miss Etta Cone
of Baltimore, Maryland,
BMA 1950.12.481

With Claribel thoroughly involved in her medical career, Etta undertook her first trip to Europe in 1901. She was joined by Gertrude and Leo Stein, who had lived for a time in Baltimore during the previous decade. Like Claribel, Gertrude had studied at the Johns Hopkins Medical School, but abandoned the pursuit of a medical career in 1902, moving to Paris to live with her brother. Through the Stein family, the Cones met Matisse and Picasso and shortly thereafter began to acquire works by both artists (FIGURE 12).

Etta appears to have made most of the purchases in the early years, buying her first oil, Matisse's *Yellow Pottery from Provence*, in 1906, the year in which it was painted. It is possible that this still life was briefly in the collection of Gertrude Stein. The Cones would consistently procure works from the Steins, whose tastes generally paralleled their own. The most significant acquisition in this regard was Matisse's fauve masterpiece from 1907, *The Blue Nude*, bought by Claribel at the John Quinn sale in Paris in October 1926. It had belonged to Leo Stein until about 1913. Other ex-Stein collection works include Marie Laurencin's *Group of Artists*, 1908 (no. 54), acquired by Claribel in 1925, Cézanne's small composition *Bathers*, 1898/1900, and Picasso's Blue Period *Woman with Bangs*, 1902 (no. 52), both bought by Etta, in 1926 and 1929/30 respectively. Neither of the Cone sisters was enamored of Picasso's cubist works and The Cone Collection thus lacks examples of this major aspect of his production.

Prior to 1922, purchases had been made by Etta Cone alone, with the exception of a group of drawings and etchings acquired by both sisters from Picasso in 1906. Indeed, the majority of their early purchases were works on paper. With the end of World War I and Claribel's subsequent return from Germany, where she had focused her professional life, the sisters' collecting activities resumed in earnest. The Cone family textile business had flourished during the war, and the added revenue supported ambitious and more frequent purchases. Traveling abroad regularly, Claribel and Etta also began to do business with a number of art dealers, among them Bernheim Jeune in Paris and Paul Vallotton, the artist Felix's brother, in Lausanne. Following her sister's death in 1929, Etta would make numerous acquisitions at the Thannhauser Galleries in Berlin and Lucerne, Galerie Rosengart, also in Lucerne, and Paul Rosenberg's gallery in Paris.

It may have been their involvement with commercial dealers as well as the increase in their income that led the Cones gradually to broaden their interests through the 1920s. They continued to expand their Matisse holdings, purchasing no less than six paintings from Bernheim Jeune during the summer of 1922. Three years later, Claribel acquired from the same dealer Cézanne's great landscape *Mont Sainte-Victoire Seen from the Bibémus Quarry*, ca. 1897 (no. 44), and from Paul Vallotton two canvases by Renoir (FIGURE 14). Etta's purchases in the 1920s, though perhaps somewhat more modest, included, in addition to Cézanne's small *Bathers*, paintings by Othon Coubine, Albert Marquet and, in 1928, Renoir's *Washerwomen*, ca. 1888 (no. 39), a work of which she became especially fond.

The Cone sisters' last trip abroad together took place in 1929. They traveled to Lausanne in the hope that Claribel's declining health would benefit from the temperate climate. Typically, she could not resist the purchase of four more paintings, all landscapes, including a Marquet, a Sisley, Pissarro's *The Highway* (*"La Côte de Valhermeil"*), 1880 (no. 31), and Gustave Courbet's *The Shaded Stream at Le Puits Noir*, 1860/5 (no. 25).

Claribel Cone died of pneumonia in Lausanne on 20 September 1929 at the age of 64. She left her entire collection to Etta. It is important to recognize that each sister, for the most part, made acquisitions independent of the other, and they considered their respective holdings as discrete entities. Indeed, they maintained separate living quarters in The Marlborough on Eutaw Place in Baltimore, where they each displayed their collections. In her will, written only months before her death, Claribel expressed the hope that, should "the spirit of appreciation for modern art" in the city improve, Etta would bequeath their combined collections to The Baltimore Museum of Art.

Throughout the 1930s, Etta continued to expand the breadth of the collection with a remarkable series of diverse purchases. Among the more notable acquisitions were Van Gogh's *Landscape with Figures*, 1889 (no. 46), a complement to the artist's moving still life *A Pair of Boots*, 1887 (no. 45), acquired by Claribel from Paul Vallotton, Lucerne, in 1927, Henri Rousseau's *View of the Quai d'Ivry near the Port à l'Anglais, Seine*, 1900 (no. 50), and Paul Gauguin's monumental *Vahine no te vi* (*Woman of the Mango*), 1892 (no. 47). These works, as well as Picasso's *Mother and Child*, 1922 (no. 53), were purchased from Galerie Rosengart, also in Lucerne.

For Etta, these years were also marked by an especially close relationship with Henri Matisse, who included a visit to Baltimore in the course of a sojourn to the United States late in 1930 (FIGURE 16). She would purchase a wide range of works by him, including a significant number of bronze sculptures, as well as drawings and prints. Among the latter was a group of over 200 graphic studies related to his illustrations for the book *Poésies de Stéphane Mallarmé*, published in 1932.

FIGURE 13 *Claribel Cone*, ca. 1927/9
photograph
(The Baltimore Museum of Art,
Cone Archives)

FIGURE 14 *Claribel Cone's Apartment,
The Marlborough Apartments,*
Baltimore, December 1930
(with Cézanne's *Mont Sainte-Victoire*
hanging on right)
photograph
(The Baltimore Museum of Art,
Cone Archives)

FIGURE 15 *Etta Cone*, 1930s
photograph
(The Baltimore Museum of Art,
Cone Archives)

PLATE 1 Henri Matisse
(French, 1869–1954)
The Yellow Dress, 1929/31
oil on canvas
The Baltimore Museum of Art
The Cone Collection, formed by
Dr Claribel and Miss Etta Cone
of Baltimore, Maryland,
BMA 1950.256

However, it was Etta's spectacular selection of Matisse paintings, acquired in the 1930s during annual summer visits abroad, that greatly enriched the collection. In 1932, she purchased *The Yellow Dress*, 1929/31 (PLATE 1), which was followed two years later by the large composition *Interior with Dog*, 1934. Like *The Blue Eyes*, 1935, it was acquired the year in which it was painted, and, in 1936, Etta bought *Large Reclining Nude (The Pink Nude)*, 1935 (PLATE 2). Not long after this last purchase, the artist sent her a group of 22 photographs taken between 3 May and 30 October 1935 in which he recorded the transformation of the image from a more conventional composition into a bold, highly decorative finished work. In 1937, the year before her final journey to Europe, Etta augmented her holdings once again with *Purple Robe and Anemones*, 1937 (no. 57), and *Odalisque with Green Sash*, 1927 (no. 56), painted some ten years earlier.

The nature of the relationship between Etta Cone and Henri Matisse is perhaps best demonstrated in a letter from July 1933 that Etta wrote to her brother, Frederic Cone, following a call on the artist in Nice:

> My visit was a joy he said. . . . I have a surprise for you, & presently I turned & there sat the model in the yellow taffeta dress with the large yellow hat on, just in front of the window—the exact reproduction of my latest painting [*The Yellow Dress*]. His bed-room (which is his studio when he is well) was the scene of his picture. Needless to say, I was thrilled.[25]

In the final decade of her life, Etta, now in her 70s, continued to strengthen aspects of the collection on a regular basis, purchasing mainly from New York dealers. The significant acquisitions made at this time include Corot's *The Artist's Studio*, 1865/8 (no. 10), and Matisse's *Two Girls, Red and Green Background*, from 1947, the final painting by the artist to enter the collection. It was acquired from his son, Pierre Matisse, who had established a gallery in New York less than six months before Etta Cone's death on 31 August 1949.

In accordance with Claribel's desire, The Baltimore Museum of Art received the combined collections as well as funds to build a wing for the bequest, which opened to the public in 1957. Some 20 years earlier, Etta had published a catalogue of the sisters' holdings, which she dedicated to Claribel. The Foreword, written by Dr George Boas, philosopher, professor at the Johns Hopkins University and for several years a trustee of the Museum, eloquently described Claribel and Etta Cone's collection ideology:

> There was never in the minds of the Misses Cone a desire to rival the great museums. There was simply a

desire to own those specific pictures which pleased their sense of beauty. Their collection therefore is as much a testimony of themselves as of the history of art. The brilliance of Dr Cone's perception, those flashes of wit, those penetrating observations which made her so engaging a conversationalist, are personified by the pictures hanging on her walls and when one enters her apartment one still feels the personality of its owner as if she were about to greet one in person. Her taste ran to power rather than to serenity; it was she who acquired the examples of Matisse's *fauve* period. Her sister's selections, on the other hand, seem to a spectator, to be of a quieter and more classic type. Her taste leads her to works of art beyond the phases of exper-imentation, to pictures which have already reached the point indicated, almost attained, in the canvases which belonged to Dr Cone. The result is that the entire collection is extremely well rounded, neither too rough nor too smooth. If one may use a musical metaphor, every suspended chord is resolved and yet there is no monotony.[26]

Recalling the 1890s, Saidie A. May (1879–1951) remembered watching from her family house in East Baltimore as Claribel Cone and Gertrude Stein walked to and from the Johns Hopkins Medical School.[27] At the time, there was little reason to anticipate that she herself would become one of the city's most notable collectors, acquiring works ranging from Egyptian antiquities to paintings and sculptures representing the avant-garde School of Paris (FIGURE 17).[28] She would also be an early supporter of such Americans as Jackson Pollock, William Baziotes and Robert Motherwell. In the period 1925 to 1931, she purchased a small number of late nineteenth- and early twentieth-century French paintings, including works by Renoir, Bonnard, Utrillo and Georges Seurat's pointillist oil sketch painted at Honfleur in 1886 (no. 42). An exceptionally altruistic benefactor, Saidie May, in her selections, especially in the modern field, endeavored to complement rather than duplicate existing holdings in the city. Ultimately, she presented more than 300 works of art to The Baltimore Museum of Art.

Jacob Blaustein (1892–1970) might more aptly be described as a connoisseur rather than as a collector. The Baltimore industrialist, who, together with his father, developed a modest kerosene delivery business into the American Oil Company, led a strenuous pace pursuing various business interests. Blaustein also served as a consultant to five United States presidents from

FIGURE 16 *Henri Matisse in Etta Cone's Dining Room, The Marlborough Apartments,* Baltimore, 1939 photograph (The Baltimore Museum of Art, Cone Archives)

PLATE 2 Henri Matisse
(French, 1869–1954)
Large Reclining Nude
(*The Pink Nude*), 1935
oil on canvas
The Baltimore Museum of Art
The Cone Collection,
formed by Dr Claribel and
Miss Etta Cone of Baltimore,
Maryland, BMA 1950.258

Franklin Delano Roosevelt to Lyndon Johnson, and promoted numerous causes, especially those pertaining to human rights and to the United Nations. Despite these activities, he found time to study music, cultivate orchids and to acquire a few paintings of exceptional quality for his estate "Alto Dale," in the northern outskirts of the city. In addition to superb portraits by Benjamin West and John Singleton Copley, Blaustein owned a number of works in various mediums by French nineteenth- and early twentieth-century artists. His most celebrated acquisition, Paul Gauguin's portrait of a cello player, entitled *Upaupa Schneklud*, 1894, was presented to the Baltimore Museum by his widow in 1979 (no. 48).

Even in this summary of collecting French art in Baltimore, a pattern seems to emerge. From the early nineteenth century, when the city began to develop as a major commercial center, it attracted and ultimately sustained a substantial merchant class. With their new fortunes, some of the city's most prosperous residents cultivated a taste for the fine arts, both acquiring the art of the past and patronizing talents of their own eras. Some preferred to support American artists, while others looked abroad. From the mid-nineteenth century, Paris, the international capital of the art world, consistently attracted wealthy Baltimoreans. The presence of George Lucas during these years provided a unique entrée into the lively market. Although in retrospect the tastes of these individuals may appear conservative, they were nonetheless supporting contemporary artists.

In the early decades of this century, the Cone sisters and Saidie A. May, although still drawn to the art of the past, made their greatest contributions as discerning collectors of the work of their contemporaries. Others, like Henry Walters, Mary Frick Jacobs and Jacob Epstein, consistently favored the art of previous eras, much as Robert Gilmor, Jr had a hundred years earlier. Remarkably, many of their magnificent collections remained essentially intact and, in acts of philanthropy rarely equaled, were given to the citizens of Baltimore for their edification and pleasure.

FIGURE 17 Othon Friesz
(French, 1869–1949)
Portrait of Saidie May, 1937
oil on canvas
The Baltimore Museum of Art
Bequest of Saidie A. May
BMA 1951.301

Paul Gauguin
(French, 1848–1903)
Upaupa Schneklud (The Player Schneklud), 1894 (detail)
oil on canvas
The Baltimore Museum of Art
Given by Hilda K. Blaustein, in Memory of her late Husband, Jacob Blaustein, BMA 1979.163

CATALOGUE

1

Marguerite Gérard

Grasse, 1761–Paris, 1837

Family Group, ca. 1810/20

oil on canvas

32 x 25½ in (81.3 x 65.8 cm)

Inscribed: *Mte Gérard*

The Baltimore Museum of Art

Gift of Billy Baldwin, BMA 1959.23

Although born in Grasse in southern France, Marguerite Gérard, the daughter of a perfume manufacturer, spent much of her life in Paris, where she became the protégé of her brother-in-law, the rococo artist Jean-Honoré Fragonard. Her study of the art of the past, especially the genre scenes painted by such Dutch masters as Terborch and Metsu, provided the basis for her own compositions, which reveal the informal and sometimes intimate aspects of contemporary upper-class French life.

Gérard's subjects are often family groups shown in elegantly appointed interiors. The details of the furnishings, costumes and accessories are carefully rendered in a highly finished manner. Frequently, she portrays women and children casually posed and engaged in pleasurable pursuits.

The individuals in this painting have not been identified. A child of eight or nine, restraining a dog, stands before a fashionably dressed middle-aged couple. The accessories of the woman's attire, especially her jewelry, are carefully noted, and the fabric of her empire-style gown is exquisitely rendered. Behind the group, a circular table with books and an armchair, both in the neoclassical style of the period, describe the interior setting.

By 1785, Gérard's fame was firmly established and she enjoyed a reputation as one of France's leading women artists. From the 1790s, when the salons were opened to women, she exhibited on a regular basis. In the course of these exhibitions, she was awarded three medals, and both Napoleon and Louis XVIII purchased her paintings.

Marguerite Gérard never married, preferring to devote herself to her art. A painter of portraits and miniatures as well as domestic genre, she attained considerable financial success. After the deaths of Fragonard, her sister, Marie Anne, and others in the family, she presided over the care of their various children and grandchildren.

2

Jean-Auguste-Dominique Ingres

Montauban, 1780–Paris, 1867

The Betrothal of Raphael and the Niece of Cardinal Bibbiena,
1813/14

oil on paper mounted on canvas

23³⁄₈ x 18¼ in (59.36 x 46.3 cm)

Inscribed: *INGRES*

The Walters Art Gallery, 37.13

Purchased by Henry Walters, 1903

Even though many of his paintings display romantic overtones,
Ingres is generally regarded as the last major representative of
the classical tradition in French painting. After training in the
studio of the neoclassical artist Jacques-Louis David, Ingres won
the Prix de Rome in 1801, entitling him to study for four years at
the Académie de France in Rome. Rather than returning to Paris
at the end of his term at the Académie, he remained in Italy
until 1820.

In 1813, King Joachim Murat of Naples and his wife, Caroline
(Napoleon's sister), commissioned Ingres to produce several
paintings, including this small genre scene, *The Betrothal of
Raphael*, completed by the artist over a 20-day period. It was
one of a number of subjects from the life of Raphael that Ingres
planned to paint, but one of the few that he completed. Cardinal
Bibbiena, Raphael's life-long friend, is portrayed as he presents
to the artist his niece, who unfortunately would die before the
marriage could transpire. Ingres based his likeness of Raphael
on an image once thought to be a self-portrait, but which has
since been identified as that of the artist's friend, Bindo Altoviti
(Samuel H. Kress Collection, National Gallery of Art, Washington,
D.C.), and for the cardinal he drew on Raphael's portrait of
Bibbiena in the Pitti Palace, Florence.

Five works on paper can be related to this painting. In an
early drawing in the Musée du Louvre and in a late gouache in
the Fogg Art Museum (Cambridge, Massachussetts), Ingres
replaced the half-draped doorway with an open window
providing a view of the Vatican and of old St Peter's basilica.

3

Jean-Auguste-Dominique Ingres

Montauban, 1780–Paris, 1867

Oedipus and the Sphinx, 1864

oil on canvas

41½ x 34¼ in (105.5 x 86.9 cm)

Inscribed: *J Ingres fbat/etatis/LXXXIII/1864*

The Walters Art Gallery, 37.9

Purchased by Henry Walters, 1909

As told by the second-century Athenian writer Apollodorus in
The Library (III, V.8), the citizens of Thebes had been terrorized
by the Sphinx, in Greek mythology a monster with a lion's body
and the torso and head of a woman. She devoured whoever
failed to solve the riddle: "What is that which has one voice and
yet becomes four-footed, two-footed and three-footed?" When
the hero Oedipus correctly responded that "it is man, for as a
babe he is four-footed, going on four limbs, as an adult he is
two-footed and as an old man he gets a third support in a staff,"
the Sphinx, in fury, dashed herself to pieces on the rocks below.

Throughout his career, Ingres returned to earlier compositions, reworking them and producing variations. He first
depicted this subject in 1808 as a demonstration of his mastery
of the classical male figure (Paris, Musée du Louvre) while he
was at the Académie de France in Rome. In the Walters painting,
the last of the four versions, Ingres sought to refine the composition by reversing the direction in which the figures face and by
intensifying their gestures and expressions.

4

Ferdinand-Victor-Eugène Delacroix

Charenton-Saint-Maurice, 1798–Paris, 1863

Sketch for the Battle of Poitiers, 1829/30

oil on canvas

20½ x 25½ in (52 x 64.8 cm)

Inscribed: *ED*

The Walters Art Gallery, 37.110

Purchased by Henry Walters, 1899

Even though he thought of himself as a classical painter, Delacroix is regarded as the foremost exponent of the romantic movement in French art during the first half of the nineteenth century. He derived inspiration from such past masters as Peter Paul Rubens and Paolo Veronese, and in contrast to his arch-rival, Ingres, he emphasized color rather than line as his principal vehicle of expression.

In late 1829, just prior to the fall of the Bourbon monarchy, the Duchesse de Berry, Charles X's daughter-in-law, commissioned a work depicting this tragic episode in the French royal history. King John the Good of France and his 14-year-old son, the future Philip the Bold of Burgundy, are shown as they are being captured at the Battle of Poitiers (1356) by Edward, Prince of Wales, also known as the Black Prince. The larger finished painting (Paris, Musée du Louvre) differs from the more spontaneously rendered Walters preliminary sketch in that the banners are dramatically silhouetted against the horizon. Both versions illustrate the artist's concern for capturing the atmospheric effects of the light breaking through the clouds.

5
Ferdinand-Victor-Eugène Delacroix
Charenton-Saint-Maurice, 1798–Paris, 1863
Christ on the Cross, 1846
oil on canvas
31½ x 25¼ in (80 x 64.1 cm)
Inscribed: *Eug. Delacroix 1846*
The Walters Art Gallery, 37.62

Purchased by William T. Walters, 1886

By choosing novel subjects and interpreting them in a highly
personal manner, Delacroix sought to reinvigorate the tradition
of history painting that had dominated French art since the
establishment of the Académie Royale de Peinture et de
Sculpture in Paris in 1648. He was not a practicing Christian,
but he drew upon the New Testament for subjects, frequently
selecting those that dealt with Christ's Passion. It is open to
speculation whether he was attracted by the drama of these
events or was endeavoring to cope with issues of personal
faith, particularly with the dual nature of Christ—the divine and
the human.

In this painting, the expiring Christ is sharply illuminated
against the darkening sky. Two mounted Roman soldiers with
billowing banners appear on the right, and cropped at the left
are a pair of gesticulating spectators. The uplifted faces of other
onlookers are discernible in the mid-ground. Critics at the Paris
Salon in 1847 were exceptionally enthusiastic in their praise of
this particular work, noting its affinities to the paintings of Peter
Paul Rubens.

6

Ferdinand-Victor-Eugène Delacroix

Charenton-Saint-Maurice, 1798–Paris, 1863

Christ on the Sea of Galilee, 1854

oil on canvas

23½ x 28⅞ in (59.8 x 73.3 cm)

Inscribed: *Eug. Delacroix 1854*

The Walters Art Gallery, 37.186

Purchased by William T. Walters, 1889

While five apostles struggle to control a sailboat floundering in a tumultuous sea, a sixth awakens Christ, who has fallen asleep, seemingly oblivious to their peril. Light breaking through the threatening clouds reveals a forbidding rocky coast in the background.

Delacroix painted a series of works illustrating this dramatic incident from the Gospels (Matthew 8:23–7, Mark 4:36–41 and Luke 8:23–5), the earliest dating from about 1840/5 (Kansas City, Nelson Atkins Museum of Art) and the last being the Walters version from 1854. In this example, the most elaborate in the series, a two-masted sailboat is shown, whereas in a version in Zurich (E. G. Bürhle Foundation) it is one-masted and in the others the vessel is a rowboat.

7

Antoine-Louis Barye

Paris, 1795–Paris, 1875

Tiger at Rest

oil on canvas

19¼ x 44⅞ in (48.9 x 114 cm)

Inscribed: *BARYE*

The Walters Art Gallery, 37.833

Purchased by William T. Walters, 1884

Barye, the foremost *animalier* of the nineteenth century, is remembered for large sculptures and numerous editions of small bronzes, but he also painted watercolors, which he exhibited at the Paris salons from 1831 until 1834. However, little is known of his oil paintings, which were only discovered in his studio after his death.

Barye had trained with the early romantic painter Antoine-Jean Gros as well as with the neoclassical sculptor François-Joseph Bosio. In the late 1820s, he and Eugène Delacroix sketched together at the Jardin des Plantes (Paris zoo) and also at the royal menagerie at Saint-Cloud. He later became closely associated with the artists who gathered at the Auberge Ganne, an inn in the village of Barbizon on the edge of the Forest of Fontainebleau.

This painting, which is ranked as one of his largest and most spectacular, shows a reclining tiger juxtaposed against the rocky, sandy terrain distinctive of the Gorges d'Apremont, in the Forest of Fontainebleau. The manner in which Barye builds up the rich, pasty layers of pigments has been likened to the laborious process in which he developed the patinas on his bronze sculptures.

8

Jean-Baptiste-Camille Corot

Paris, 1796–Paris, 1875

Sèvres-Brimborion, View towards Paris, 1858/64

oil on canvas

18³⁄₈ x 24¼ in (46.7 x 61.6 cm)

Inscribed: *COROT*

The Baltimore Museum of Art

George A. Lucas Collection, BMA 1996.45.66

Purchased by George A. Lucas from the artist, 10 April 1864

While a student in Rome in 1824/5, Corot adopted the practice
of painting out-of-doors as a preliminary step to preparing his
"finished" paintings in his studio. Over the years, the distinction
between these two phases of his creative process would diminish
and he would find a ready market for both oil sketches and his
more fully developed studio works.

This painting is the largest of five that Corot produced,
showing the view looking down the Brancas road that ran from
Ville d'Avray, the location of the Corot family house, through
Sèvres and the district of Brimborion on the Seine River, toward
Paris, discernible in the distance in the east. Of the other versions,
which differ most obviously in the placing of the figures on the
road, one is preserved in The Metropolitan Museum of Art in
New York and another was until recently in the Musée du Louvre,
Paris. The whereabouts of the remaining two are unknown. With
the exception of one of the last two missing paintings, which was
listed as a morning scene, and lacked the shadows extending
across the road in the foreground, these works portray the same
site at varying times of the afternoon and under slightly differing
conditions of light and atmosphere. In his interest in capturing
such ephemeral effects, Corot anticipated the impressionist
landscape painters, most notably Alfred Sisley, who also portrayed
similar road scenes looking toward Paris.

9

Jean-Baptiste-Camille Corot

Paris, 1796–Paris, 1875

The Evening Star, 1864

oil on canvas

28 x 35³⁄₈ in (71 x 90 cm)

Inscribed: *COROT*

The Walters Art Gallery, 37.154

Commissioned from the artist by William T. Walters, 1864

In the 1850s, Corot gradually turned from the bright, clearly
defined landscapes of his earlier years to more subtle, poetic
works, sometimes known as "souvenirs," in which he sought
to record not only his visual experience of the site, but also to
convey the sensations evinced by it. Employing a restricted
range of colors, he now emphasized tonal harmonies.

During a visit to the artist's studio in February, 1864,
William Walters so admired *L'Étoile du berger* (Toulouse, Musée
des Augustins), then in the process of being painted, that he
commissioned this replica which is reduced in scale. It is thought
that the subject had been inspired by lines from Alfred de
Musset's poem *The Willow: Fragment* (1830):

> Pale Star of the evening, distant messenger,
> Whose countenance is brilliant like the rays of sunset,
> From your azure palace to the depths of the firmament,
> What are you looking at on the plain?

10

Jean-Baptiste-Camille Corot

Paris, 1796–Paris, 1875

The Artist's Studio, ca. 1865/8

oil on panel

16 x 13 in (40.6 x 33 cm)

Inscribed: *COROT*

The Baltimore Museum of Art

The Cone Collection, formed by Dr Claribel Cone and

Miss Etta Cone of Baltimore, Maryland, BMA 1950.200

Between 1865 and 1870, Corot produced six paintings entitled *The Artist's Studio*. In the Baltimore painting, as well as in versions in the National Gallery of Art, Washington, D.C., and in the Musée du Louvre, Paris, a model wearing an Italian peasant costume is shown from the back in three-quarters view. She is seated in front of an easel in the artist's Paris studio. This intimate interior scene with its suffused lighting, recalls paintings by the seventeenth-century Delft master Jan Vermeer, who only recently had been rediscovered by French connoisseurs.

The Baltimore version, rendered in loose, fluid brushstrokes, is the most vibrant of the three. Recent scholarship suggests that it is an *ébauche*, or preliminary study, for the larger Washington painting, whereas the Louvre painting is a later variant. The oil sketch on the easel has been identified as the now lost *Ville-d'Avray: A Cluster of Trees*.

Jean-Baptiste-Camille Corot
Paris, 1796–Paris, 1875
The Crown of Flowers, 1865/70
oil on canvas
25½ x 17 in (64.8 x 43.2 cm)
Inscribed: *COROT*
The Baltimore Museum of Art
The Helen and Abram Eisenberg Collection, 1968, BMA 1968.36

Purchased by Mrs Abram Eisenberg from Knoedler & Co.,
New York, March 1925

Seeking to disprove to his critics that his talents were limited to
landscape painting, Corot produced a number of paintings of
single figures, especially during the late 1860s and early 1870s,
although only four of them were exhibited in his lifetime. His
figure paintings are imbued with classical overtones and a
distinctive solemnity, qualities that have led scholars to draw
affinities between them and the works of both Raphael and
Rembrandt, as well as other great masters of the past.

A model, who has been identified as "Cécile," is depicted
full-length and in three-quarters view, seated at the edge of a
path, apparently lost in reverie as she weaves a crown of flowers.
The sprig of flowers in her hair and her Italian costume with its
dark outer garment trimmed in pink, and her dress with its blue
and white zigzag design, impart notes of color to this painting,
unusual for Corot's later works, which are usually rendered in
muted tones.

Jean-Baptiste-Camille Corot

Paris, 1796–Paris, 1875

Shepherds of Arcadia, ca. 1872

oil on canvas

31 x 35⅝ in (78.7 x 90.5 cm)

Inscribed: *COROT*

The Baltimore Museum of Art

Bequest of Jacob Epstein, BMA 1951.106

Purchased by Jacob Epstein from Knoedler & Co., Paris, 1921

In the late landscapes painted in his studio, Corot drew upon his recollections of various sites he had frequented in the past, including Lake Nemi near Rome and Ville d'Avray and Mortefontaine outside Paris, synthesizing them to create sylvan vistas rendered in distinctive silvery tones. He usually populated these bucolic reveries with the same bacchantes and shepherds, and shepherdesses with their sheep who inhabited the ancient Arcady of Nicolas Poussin and Claude Lorrain.

To convey his impressions of light and atmospheric effects at varying times of the day, often at dawn or dusk, Corot adopted a highly personal, varied technique combining transparent washes, impasto and daubs of paint applied with individual brushstrokes or with a palette knife.

Shepherds of Arcadia was among the paintings featured in a memorial exhibition held in Paris in the École des Beaux-Arts after the artist's death.

13

Pierre-Etienne-Théodore Rousseau

Paris, 1812–Barbizon, 1867

Effet de Givre, 1845

oil on canvas

25 x 38⅝ in (63.5 x 98 cm)

The Walters Art Gallery, 37.25

Purchased by William T. Walters, 1882

Among the members of the Barbizon school, Rousseau is regarded as the foremost exponent of pure landscape painting. After training briefly in the studio of the historical landscape painter Joseph Rémond, he turned to copying the works of the seventeenth-century artists, notably Claude Lorrain and the Van de Velde brothers, and he was also profoundly impressed by the landscapes of the English artist John Constable. From his youth, Rousseau had sketched directly from nature. He began to explore the countryside and, as early as 1827/8, he painted in the Forest of Fontainebleau.

Rousseau completed *Effet de Givre* over the course of eight days while staying with his colleague, Jules Dupré, at L'Isle-Adam on the Oise River during the winter of 1845/6. This painting represented a radical departure for the artist, who normally maintained the distinction between the *ébauche* (oil sketch) painted directly from nature and the definitive work prepared in the studio. He has captured the effect of the golden light breaking through the clouds to illuminate the hoarfrost glistening on the rocky terrain.

14

Constant Troyon

Sèvres, 1810–Paris, 1865

Coast near Villers, about 1859

oil on canvas

26½ x 37¾ in (67.4 x 95.7 cm)

The Walters Art Gallery, 37.993

Purchased by Henry Walters, 1903

Troyon represented the third generation of his family to be employed at Sèvres decorating porcelain. In his spare time, he sketched in the Forest of Fontainebleau, where he encountered the landscape painter Camille Roqueplan, who, in turn, introduced him to Théodore Rousseau. Troyon decided to leave Sèvres and to devote himself to painting, and, in 1833, he began to exhibit landscapes recalling his travels to the various regions of the country. Troyon often introduced animals into his compositions, but it was only after he had seen the works of the Dutch seventeenth-century masters Paulus Potter and Albertus Cuyp, during a visit to the Netherlands and Belgium in 1847, that he decided to specialize in animal genre painting.

An inscription on the stretcher of this work identifies the site as the coastal resort village of Villers-sur-Mer in the Calvados department of France. Troyon employed a low horizon to dramatize the sky, seen as a storm moves inland threatening to obscure the sunlight piercing the clouds. Various walks of life are represented, including a peasant couple riding on ponies equipped with panniers, a sportsman strolling with his gun and hunters setting up fowling nets.

15

Virgile Narcisse Diaz de la Peña

Bordeaux, 1807–Menton, 1876

Forest of Fontainebleau, Autumn, 1871

oil on panel

$30^{3}/_{4}$ x $25^{3}/_{8}$ in (78 x 64.7 cm)

Inscribed: *N. Diaz. 71*

The Walters Art Gallery, 37.64

Purchased by William T. Walters, before 1878

Following the early deaths of his Spanish parents in Bordeaux, Diaz was reared by a Protestant minister in Bellevue outside Paris. His training was limited to experience as an apprentice-decorator at a porcelain manufactory and time spent copying Old Masters at the Musée du Louvre. As early as 1835, he began to explore the Forest of Fontainebleau, and it was at the Auberge Ganne, in Barbizon, on the edge of the forest, that he befriended other painters who would come to be identified as members of the Barbizon school. Diaz specialized in forest interiors, often incorporating figurative motifs, including gypsies and ancient goddesses, executed in a manner recalling the eighteenth-century rococo style.

In this late work, however, Diaz has dispensed with any references to humans and focuses instead on an ancient tree with broken limbs at the edge of a clearing. He achieves a tapestry-like effect by dabbling and scumbling his pigments in rich russets, ochre, yellows and olive tints. As a genial individual, and as the most daring colorist of the Barbizon painters, he was particularly admired by the future impressionists Monet, Sisley and Renoir.

16

Jean-François Millet

Gruchy, 1814–Barbizon, 1875

The Potato Harvest, 1855

oil on canvas

21¼ x 25⅞ in (54 x 65.2 cm)

Inscribed: *J.F. Millet*

The Walters Art Gallery, 37.115

Purchased by William T. Walters, before 1878

Millet was born into a peasant family in the hamlet of Gruchy in Normandy. Although he was the most widely cultured of the painters associated with the Barbizon school, being thoroughly versed in both French and foreign literature and steeped in the classical traditions of French art, Millet took pride in remaining true to his peasant background. After receiving instruction in Cherbourg, he left Normandy for Paris in 1837 to enroll in the studio of the academic teacher Paul Delaroche. Discouraged by his failure to win the Prix de Rome and by his limited success at the Paris salons, Millet withdrew to Normandy in 1840. Only after his return to Paris five years later did he begin to establish friendships with Constant Troyon, Narcisse Diaz, Charles Jacque and Théodore Rousseau, who would become his companions in Barbizon. He settled in the village in the summer of 1849, after an outbreak of cholera in Paris threatened the safety of his family. What distinguished him from his Barbizon colleagues was his singular commitment to figurative painting.

Millet keenly felt the profound changes affecting agrarian society in mid-nineteenth-century France and the hardships they imposed on rural laborers. In this painting, he imparts a dignity and a grandeur to the toiling peasants by depicting them on a monumental scale.

17

Jean-François Millet

Gruchy, 1814–Barbizon, 1875

The Sheepfold, Moonlight, 1856/60

oil on panel

17⅞ x 24¹⁵⁄₁₆ in (45.3 x 63.4 cm)

Inscribed: *J.F. MILLET*

The Walters Art Gallery, 37.30

Purchased by William T. Walters, between 1878 and 1887

In the mid-1850s, Millet began to give greater prominence in his compositions to landscape settings. He produced several works related to this nocturnal scene. The waning moon throws a soft, mysterious light across the plain extending between the villages of Barbizon and Chailly, and dissolves the forms in the foreground. A realist, Millet chose his subjects from the most humble ranks of the social order. Itinerant shepherds led solitary existences, living in small wagons and keeping their herds in portable pens.

18

Jean-François Millet

Gruchy, 1814–Barbizon, 1875

The Goose Girl, ca. 1863

oil on canvas

15½ x 18¼ in (39.3 x 46.5 cm)

The Walters Art Gallery, 37.153

Purchased by Henry Walters, 1905

An adolescent girl seated on the bank of a stream dangles her foot in the water. Her sabots and clothing are stashed behind her against a tree trunk. This woodland scene is animated by the gaggle of geese upstream and a pair of cows visible through an opening at the right. A slow, deliberate painter, Millet had begun to develop this subject over seven years earlier, as is demonstrated by a preliminary drawing, *Study for "The Goose Girl Bathing,"* of about 1854/5 (Princeton, New Jersey, The Art Museum, Princeton University). Sunlight penetrating the foliage picks out individual elements, bathing them in a warm glow, thereby unifying the composition. This painting has been described as "one of the most beautifully integrated scenes of a bather in a landscape by a nineteenth-century painter." Camille Pissarro, who was a fervent admirer of Millet's work, produced a variant, *Woman Washing her Feet* (New York, The Metropolitan Museum of Art).

19

Charles-François Daubigny
Paris, 1817–Paris, 1878
On the Oise, 1868
oil on wood panel
15 x 26 in (38.1 x 66 cm)
Inscribed: *Daubigny 1868*
The Baltimore Museum of Art
The Helen and Abram Eisenberg Collection, BMA 1976.55.2

Daubigny was born into a family of artists and began to draw and paint in his youth, frequently working at Saint-Cloud and Clamart in the environs of Paris as well as in the Forest of Fontainebleau. Following a six-month sojourn in Italy, he began to produce illustrations for books and magazines, an activity that sustained him for several years.

Daubigny first exhibited at the Paris Salon in 1838 and would continue to submit works until 1868. He rose to prominence only after 1850. Excursions in the French countryside in the company of his close friend Camille Corot, reinforced his commitment to paint landscapes directly from nature. Drawn especially to the rivers of France, he explored the Seine, Marne and Oise waterways, using a studio-boat, "Le Botin," which he moored when a particular vista pleased him. A generation later, an admirer Claude Monet, would adopt a similar method of working from a small boat when painting the Seine River and its tributaries at Giverny.

In the late 1850s, Daubigny's success was assured when the French government purchased a number of his landscapes and commissioned decorative works as well. Although criticized by some for his renditions of the transitory aspects of nature, which were referred to merely as "sketches barely begun," other critics, like Zacharie Astruc, would praise him: "He is *the* painter of simple impressions. He is tender; he is sweet; he is captivating. One feels that he profoundly loves the beautiful freshness . . . [the] . . . deep clear waters so well rendered their poetic grace by his brush."

Daubigny's influence was far-reaching. Among his pupils were Eugène Boudin and Johan Barthold Jongkind. While in exile in London during the Franco-Prussian War (1870/1), he would introduce younger colleagues, Camille Pissarro and Claude Monet, to his dealer, Paul Durand-Ruel. After his death in February 1878, and, in accordance with his wishes, he was buried next to his old friend Corot at the Cemetery of Père Lachaise in Paris.

20

Jules-Adolphe-Aimé-Louis Breton
Courrières, 1827–Paris, 1906
Returning from the Fields, 1871
oil on canvas
27³/₈ x 41 in (69.5 x 104 cm)
Inscribed: *Jules Breton 1871*
The Walters Art Gallery, 37.58

Purchased by William T. Walters, 1886

Breton was reared in Courrières in the Pas de Calais department
of northern France and retained throughout his career a commitment to his native locale. After receiving an academic training in
Belgium, in Ghent and Antwerp, he completed his studies in Paris
under Michel-Martin Drölling. As a result of the 1848 Revolution
in France, Breton became financially distressed and was forced
to earn a livelihood. He initially dealt with rural subjects, in which
he conveyed a keen awareness of the plight of the peasants,
but in his later works he tended to romanticize their existence,
gain-ing popular success, but also incurring the scorn of the
realist critics.

In *Returning from the Fields*, three barefoot young women,
weary but not overcome by their labors, wend their way homeward.
Stalks of wheat and poppies line their path through the field.

21

Marc-Charles-Gabriel Gleyre

Chevilly, Switzerland, 1806–Paris, 1874

Lost Illusions, 1865/7

oil on canvas

34¼ x 59¼ in (86.5 x 150.5 cm)

The Walters Art Gallery, 37.184

Commissioned by William T. Walters, 1865

From the age of nine, Gleyre lived in France. He perfected his painting technique in the studio of Louis Hersent and took classes with the English watercolorist R. P. Bonnington.

A defining experience in his career was an extended journey of 19 months which he made to the Near East in the company of a Bostonian, John Lowell. After his return to Paris in 1838, Gleyre adopted an academic technique for his classical paintings. At the 1843 Salon, he exhibited *Le Soir* (*The Evening*), which met with an enthusiastic reception and was acquired by the state (Paris, Musée d'Orsay). The Walters picture, which replicates this composition, was initially painted as an *ébauche* by Léon Dussart (b. 1824) and was then considerably reworked by Gleyre. It recreates a vision that Gleyre was alleged to have experienced on the banks of the Nile near Abydos on the evening of 21 March 1835. An aging poet, lost in his reveries, watches as a wondrous barque carries away his youthful dreams and illusions, personified by music-making maidens and a cupid strewing flowers.

22

Jean-Léon Gérôme

Vesoul, 1824–Paris, 1904

The Duel after the Masquerade, 1857/8

oil on canvas

15³/₈ x 22¹/₈ in (39 x 56.3 cm)

Inscribed: *J.L. GEROME*

The Walters Art Gallery, 37.51

Purchased by William T. Walters, 1859

Throughout his career, Gérôme enjoyed exceptional success both with the public and in official circles. As one of the three professors appointed to teach painting at the École des Beaux-Arts after the reforms of the school's curriculum in 1863, he was in a favorable position to influence the careers of his many pupils. However, Gérôme had the misfortune to outlive the fashion for his paintings and he would be remembered by succeeding generations for his vociferous opposition to the impressionists rather than for his brilliant compositions.

In *The Duel after the Masquerade*, Gérôme presents a contemporary scene in which the protagonists, still wearing their costumes from the previous evening, have met at dawn on a snowy morning in the Bois de Boulogne. Typically, the artist presents not the event itself, but its consequences. Mortally wounded, Pierrot succumbs in the arms of the Duc de Guise while the Venetian Doge examines him. Domino, over-come by grief, clasps his head. The victor, dressed as an American Indian, is led from the field by his second, Harlequin. This painting is one of two replicas that Gérôme produced of *The Departure from a Masked Ball* (1857), which was acquired by the Duc d'Aumale and is now in the Musée Condé, Chantilly, France.

23

Jean-Léon Gérôme

Vesoul, 1824–Paris, 1904

The Death of Caesar, 1867

oil on canvas

34 x 57¼ in (85 x 145.42 cm)

Inscribed: *J.L. GEROME MDCCC...*

The Walters Art Gallery, 37.884

Purchased by Henry Walters, 1917

Whether recreating scenes set in Greek and Roman antiquity or presenting exotic views of life in the Near East and North Africa, Gérôme strove for verisimilitude. In doing so, he drew on his experiences as a frequent traveler and exploited his keen powers of observation.

In *The Death of Caesar*, the artist has departed from his usual practice of depicting genre scenes of daily life in antiquity, to show instead a specific historical event. As narrated by the second-century Greek biographer Plutarch (*Brutus* XIV–XVIII), Julius Caesar was assassinated in the curia of the Theater of Pompey on the Ides of March, 44 B.C. Rather than portraying the actual event, Gérôme shows its aftermath: the body of the emperor lying outstretched at the blood-stained base of the statue of Pompey, an overturned chair and the scattered petitions denote the sequence of the events and a lone senator, dumbfounded by what has transpired, remains slumped in his seat while the assassins depart brandishing their swords. At the Paris Salon in 1859, Gérôme exhibited a precursor of this work, *The Dead Caesar*, in which only the foreshortened body of Caesar is depicted (formerly in the Corcoran Gallery of Art, Washington, D.C.).

24

Jean-Léon Gérôme

Vesoul, 1824–Paris, 1904

A Roman Slave Market, ca. 1884

oil on canvas

25³/₁₆ x 22³/₈ in (64.1 x 56.9 cm)

Inscribed: *J.L.GEROME*

The Walters Art Gallery, 37.885

Purchased by Henry Walters, 1917

Seizing an opportunity to depict sensually appealing figurative
studies, as well as to exploit the innate horror of the subject,
Gérôme produced six paintings of slave markets, three set in
Roman antiquity and the others in nineteenth-century Cairo.
Here, the slave is portrayed from the back, and, in an adroit
display of foreshortening, the artist depicts the auctioneer
leaning forward to encourage bidders. The Walters painting
is related to a larger work, *Slave Market at Rome* (dated 1884),
now in the Hermitage Museum, St Petersburg. In the latter,
the setting is approximately the same, although seen from the
opposite vantage point.

25

Gustave Courbet

Ornans, 1819–La Tour-de-Peilz, Switzerland, 1877

The Shaded Stream at Le Puits Noir, ca. 1860/5

oil on canvas

25¼ x 31⅛ in (64.2 x 79.1 cm)

Inscribed: *G. Courbet.*

The Baltimore Museum of Art

The Cone Collection, formed by Dr Claribel Cone and

Miss Etta Cone of Baltimore, Maryland, BMA 1950.202

Purchased by Claribel Cone from Paul Vallotton,
Lausanne, September 1929

Courbet, the leader of the mid-nineteenth-century realist movement in French painting, came from a well-to-do farming family
in the Jura region of eastern France. He arrived in Paris in late
1839 intent on becoming an artist. During the 1840s, he worked
in an introspective, romantic vein, but, in 1849, his art underwent
a profound transformation. In his imposing composition, *A
Burial at Ornans*, 1849/50 (Paris, Musée d'Orsay), he treated a
scene of rural life on a monumental scale normally reserved for
history painting. In this work and others, including *The Stone-
breakers*, 1849 (formerly in Dresden, Gemäldegalerie, Neue
Meister), he conveyed his passionate commitment to record
the ordinary lives of peasants and laborers, however harsh and
unappealing these images might seem. In doing so, he shocked
a public accustomed to more idealized, pleasurable subjects.

During the late 1850s and 1860s, Courbet turned increasingly
to landscape painting, frequently incorporating figures into out-
door settings or focusing exclusively on a particular terrain.
Although his peasant subjects created controversy, his pure landscapes were generally well received. This site, near Ornans, the
picturesque town where the artist was born, constantly inspired
him and he painted a number of views of the locale. A stream
surrounded by luxuriant vegetation flows from deep within a
grotto-like arrangement of cliffs and boulders. The deep green
tones of the foliage are reflected in the still water, which becomes
shallow in the foreground, exposing the rocks of the streambed.
The overall effect is one of solitude, mystery and nature revealed.

26

Thomas Couture

Senlis, 1815–Villiers-le-Bel, 1879

Day Dreams, 1859

oil on canvas

46½ x 35½ in (118 x 90.3 cm)

Inscribed: *TC 1859*

The Walters Art Gallery, 37.44

Purchased by William T. Walters, 1887

(American tour)

A schoolboy blowing bubbles slouches in a chair while at his side are his books, still strapped together, a container of soapy water and a framed mirror with a broken glass. A laurel wreath hangs on the crumbling plaster wall. This painting has been interpreted as an allegory of vanity, with the soap bubbles and the disintegrating wall denoting ephemeral existence and the wreath symbolizing glory. Tucked into the mirror is a note inscribed: "*Le Parasseux indigne de vivre*" ("The lazy one unworthy of living").

A figure blowing bubbles has been used as an allegorical reference to vanity since the sixteenth century, as seen in Hendrick Goltzius' engraving, *Quis Evadet*? (Who can evade it?). The allusion was revived during the eighteenth century in the works of Jean-Siméon Chardin.

27

Thomas Couture

Senlis, 1815–Villiers-le-Bel, 1879

Judge Going to Court, ca. 1859/60

oil on canvas

15 x 18³⁄₁₆ in (38 x 46.2 cm)

Inscribed: *T.C.*

The Walters Art Gallery, 37.1204

Purchased by Henry Walters

After failing to win the Prix de Rome on six occasions, Couture rejected the academic tradition and determined to pursue an independent course drawing inspiration from the great Venetian painters, particularly Paolo Veronese, whose works he studied in the Musée du Louvre. He evolved a personal technique entailing bright colors and expressive textures that imparted a sense of spontaneity to his work. As a teacher, Couture encouraged his students to portray contemporary life, although his own paintings often treated moralizing themes. His pupils included Edouard Manet, with whom he frequently argued, Pierre Puvis de Chavannes and a number of Americans, among them John La Farge, Eastman Johnson and Mary Cassatt.

In this sketch, a judge, weighed down by legal tomes, trudges along a village street. The pair of shields hanging over the gate in the background denotes the residence of a notary. Perhaps the flock of fowl and the turkey cock pecking for food in the roadway are a veiled reference to the figure's profession.

28

Edouard Manet

Paris, 1832–Paris, 1883

The Café-Concert, 1878/9

oil on canvas

18¹¹⁄₁₆ x 15⁷⁄₁₆ in (47.3 x 39.1 cm)

Inscribed: *Manet*

The Walters Art Gallery, 37.893

Purchased by Henry Walters, 1907

With his emphasis on portraying contemporary life and capturing the immediacy of his vision, Manet became a key figure in the development of modern painting. He shared many of the objectives of the impressionists, but declined to participate in their group shows, preferring instead to pursue his career within the context of the Paris salons.

Manet enrolled in the studio of Thomas Couture in 1850 and stayed for six years, even though he was frequently at odds with his teacher. He supplemented his training by copying earlier works of the museums in the Netherlands, the German states, Italy and later Spain. Although historical antecedents can be found for even his most controversial works, *The Picnic on the Grass* and *Olympia* (both Paris, Musée d'Orsay), these masterpieces, which are now regarded as landmarks in the evolution of Realism, were widely misunderstood by his contemporaries.

In 1878/9, Manet turned for subjects to the indoor and out-door cafés and cabarets that he and his friends frequented in Montmartre. In this painting and in several related works, most notably the *Café-Concert de Reichshoffen*, which the artist cut into two canvases, *Corner in a Café-Concert* (London, National Gallery) and *At the Café* (Winterthur, Oscar Reinhart Collection), the setting is the Café de Reichshoffen on the Boulevard Rochechouart.

Capturing the anonymity of modern urban life, Manet depicts customers from various social classes: a dissolute-looking, weary young woman smoking, a rather rakish, older gentleman sporting a top hat and a working-class couple—all seated at the counter, seemingly oblivious to one another. Behind, a barmaid takes a swig of beer, and reflected in the mirror in the background is the image of the singer known as "La Belle Polonaise."

To achieve a sense of spontaneity, Manet has applied his pigments directly to the canvas in loose, flowing strokes, leaving the ground exposed in some areas. Each individual has been cropped somewhere by the picture frame or by other figures, thus creating an effect of instantaneity not unlike a modern snapshot.

29

Camille Pissarro

Charlotte Amalie, St Thomas, Danish West
Indies, 1830–Paris, 1903
Path by the River (near La Varenne-St Hilaire), 1864
oil on canvas
22 x 18 in (55.9 x 45.7 cm)
Inscribed: *C. Pissarro 1864*
The Baltimore Museum of Art
George A. Lucas Collection, BMA 1996.45.221

In 1855, Pissarro arrived in Paris from his birthplace, St Thomas,
in the Danish West Indies. Shortly thereafter, he met Camille
Corot, whose influence, together with that of Courbet and
Daubigny, is clearly manifested in his early work.

This landscape, painted during the artist's first extended
stay in the French countryside during the mid-1860s, has been
identified as a view of La Varenne-St Hilaire, a town in the
environs of Paris. Vertical in format, the composition, master-
fully arranged, is both intimate and expansive. Figures stroll
along a path, which curves gently in the foreground. Beyond is
a river and sloping hills that meet the sky. Although still reminiscent of the Naturalism of the Barbizon school, the landscape
also anticipates Impressionism in its attention to qualities of
light and atmosphere.

30

Camille Pissarro

Charlotte Amalie, St Thomas, Danish West
Indies, 1830–Paris, 1903

Route to Versailles, Louveciennes, ca. 1869

oil on canvas

15⅛ x 18¼ in (38.4 x 46.3 cm)

Inscribed: *C. Pissarro*

The Walters Art Gallery

The George A. Lucas Collection, 1996, 37.1989

Purchased by George A. Lucas from the Paris art
dealer, Pierre-Firmin Martin, January 1870

Like his impressionist colleagues, Pissarro was keenly observant
of changes in season and their effects on the landscape. For
several of the artists, winter proved especially challenging, with
its leaden atmosphere and white snow. Throughout his career,
Pissarro would paint winter views both in Paris and in the nearby
villages where he spent much of his life.

In the months prior to his exile in England during the
Franco-Prussian War (1870/1), the artist lived at Louveciennes,
northwest of Paris. During the winter of 1869/70, together with
his friend Claude Monet, he painted a series of views of the town.
Here, he records a street scene blanketed with heavy snow. Gray
shadows play across the frozen surface and the sky has lightened
overhead, giving the landscape the faint glow of a winter sun.

Following Pissarro's departure for London, Prussian troops
occupied his house, possibly the yellow building on the left. Much
of his work from the preceding 20 years was destroyed; however,
this painting and *Path by the River* (no. 29), both purchased
shortly after their completion, are among the few early works
that survived.

31

Camille Pissarro

Charlotte Amalie, St Thomas, Danish West
Indies, 1830–Paris, 1903
The Highway ("La Côte de Valhermeil"), 1880
oil on canvas
25¼ x 31½ in (64.2 x 80 cm)
Inscribed: *C. Pissarro.80*
The Baltimore Museum of Art
The Cone Collection, formed by Dr Claribel Cone and
Miss Etta Cone of Baltimore, Maryland, BMA 1950.280

Purchased by Claribel Cone from Paul Vallotton,
Lausanne, August 1929

Around 1880, Pissarro painted a number of views of Valhermeil,
a hamlet near Pontoise northwest of Paris, where he settled
after the Franco-Prussian War (1870/1). Typically, the artist has
carefully organized his composition. A roadway with a group of
figures recedes diagonally toward the center of the landscape
and the sloping hill in the background. Clouds fill the sky and
long shadows fall across the road, suggesting that the time of
day is late afternoon. Although Pissarro would not adopt a
pointillist technique until 1885, the small, regular touches of
pigment in certain passages of this work suggest the direction
he would pursue.

32

Hilaire-Germaine-Edgar Degas
Paris, 1834–Paris, 1917
Before the Race, 1882/4
oil on laminated panel
10³/₈ x 13³/₄ in (26.4 x 34.9 cm)
Inscribed: *Degas*
The Walters Art Gallery, 37.850

Purchased by Henry Walters, 1910

Edgar Degas played a pivotal role in organizing the impressionist exhibitions and participated in all but the seventh group show. He was expansive in his views regarding the movement and welcomed such artists as Mary Cassatt, Jean-François Raffäelli and Giuseppe De Nittis, who shared his realist commitment to recording modern life. However, given the highly deliberative process by which he created his compositions, relying on recollections rather than immediate visual experience, he frequently found himself at odds with his colleagues, who stressed the importance of spontaneity and painting in the open air.

Equestrian motifs had figured in Degas' production since the outset of his career. In one of his notebooks from 1855, he drew copies of the horses on the frieze of the Parthenon and, in slightly later drawings dating from his Italian sojourn of 1856/9, he copied such fifteenth-century works as Paolo Uccello's *Battle of San Romano* (Florence, Uffizi Gallery) and Benozzo Gozzoli's *Journey of the Magi* (Florence, Palazzo Medici-Riccardi), both of which prominently featured horses. Degas not only included horses in his historical compositions of the 1860s, but he also produced a number of track and steeplechase scenes and, in doing so, he was treating one of the most popular facets of contemporary life. The racecourse at Longchamps had opened in 1857 and the Grand Prix de Paris was first run in 1863, the same year that the Société Générale des Steeple-Chases was established.

This painting, showing five jockeys and their horses positioned in a loose wedge against a summarily rendered landscape, is one of three closely related works that Degas painted in the early 1880s. The others, with the same title, are in the Sterling and Francine Clark Art Institute in Williamstown, Massachusetts, and formerly in the collection of Mrs John Hay Whitney. In the Walters version, the artist has applied the pigments so thinly as to exploit the sensuous quality of the wood.

33

(Oscar-)Claude Monet

Paris, 1840–Giverny, 1926

Windmills Near Zaandam, 1871

oil on canvas

16 x 28½ in (40.6 x 72.4 cm)

Inscribed: *Claude Monet*

The Walters Art Gallery, 37.894

Acquired by Henry Walters, after 1909

During the Franco-Prussian War (1870/1), Monet and his family sought refuge in London. Arriving in October 1870, they remained until the following May, moving on to Holland before their return to Paris in the autumn of 1871.

After stopping in Amsterdam, the Monets continued to Zaandam, a picturesque river town a few miles north of the city. In the course of their five-month sojourn, the artist painted more than 20 views of the village and its environs. In this landscape, the expansive sky and the waterway dominate the composition. A female figure carrying buckets crosses the wooden footbridge and a rower makes his way along the water's edge. Windmills silhouetted against dramatic cloud formations confirm the identity of the locale. In his landscapes produced in Holland, Monet's debt to Johan Jongkind, the Dutch painter of water views whom he had met at Le Havre in 1862, is clearly apparent.

34 and 35

(Oscar-)Claude Monet

Paris, 1840–Giverny, 1926

Waterloo Bridge ("Effect of Sun with Smoke"), 1903

oil on canvas

26 x 39¾ in (66.1 x 101 cm)

Inscribed: *Claude Monet 1903*

The Baltimore Museum of Art

The Helen and Abram Eisenberg Collection, BMA 1976.38

Acquired by Mrs Abram Eisenberg, ca. 1923

Charing Cross Bridge ("Reflections on the Thames"), 1901/4

oil on canvas

25⅝ x 39½ in (65.8 x 100.3 cm)

Inscribed: *Claude Monet*

The Baltimore Museum of Art

The Helen and Abram Eisenberg Collection, BMA 1945.94

Acquired by Mrs Abram Eisenberg, ca. 1935

(American tour)

In December 1891, Monet visited London for the third time since his exile during the Franco-Prussian War 20 years earlier. Thoroughly immersed in his series paintings, having completed the *Grainstacks* and *Poplars at Giverny*, he expressed the hope of returning to London and pursuing a similar course concentrating on the Thames River and its immediate surroundings. It was not until 1899 that his desire was fulfilled. In subsequent visits in 1900 and 1901, he began scores of canvases capturing the view from the window of his room at the Savoy Hotel on the Victoria Embankment.

In addition to the Houses of Parliament, which he painted from St Thomas's Hospital, Monet recorded his impressions of the Charing Cross and Waterloo bridges at different times of the day. Vessels with plumes of smoke coming from their stacks and tall chimneys emitting their industrial exhaust add to the thickness of the prevailing fog. Monet was especially taken with the city's dense atmosphere, which became the unifying element in his London views. He commented to an acquaintance:

> The fog in London assumes all sorts of colors; there are black, brown, yellow, green, purple fogs, and the interest in painting is to get the objects as seen through all these fogs. My practiced eye has found that objects change in appearance in a London fog more and quicker than in any other atmosphere, and the difficulty is to get every change down on canvas.

36

Alfred Sisley

Paris, 1839–Moret-sur-Loing, 1899
The Terrace at Saint-Germain: Spring, 1875
oil on canvas
29 x 39¼ in (74 x 99.6 cm)
Inscribed: *Sisley.75*
The Walters Art Gallery, 37.992

Purchased by Henry Walters, 1900

Although born in Paris, Alfred Sisley, the quintessential impressionist
landscape painter, was British. He was sent by his father to London
in 1857/9 to prepare for a career in commerce. During visits to the
National Gallery, Sisley was undoubtedly attracted to the landscapes
of John Constable and J. M. W. Turner as well as to those of the Dutch
seventeenth-century masters. Upon his return to Paris, he enrolled in
the studio of Charles Gleyre, where he befriended his future colleagues
Auguste Renoir, Frédéric Bazille and Claude Monet, whom he joined
in painting in the Forest of Fontainebleau. After his father's business
was ruined during the Franco-Prussian War (1870/1), Sisley led a
penurious existence as a painter. He exhibited six works in the first
impressionist exhibition in 1874 and was a major contributor to the
1876, 1877 and 1882 group shows.

While residing in the suburban village of Port Marly west of Paris,
Sisley painted this sweeping, panoramic view of the Seine Valley
looking west towards Saint-Germain-en-Laye, the site of France's
royal court until 1682. Despite this historical association, the artist has
introduced notes of modernity, including tugboats pulling barges and
the iron railroad bridge. He conveys the distinctive atmosphere of the
moisture-laden climate of the valley on an early spring day. In the
foreground, laborers tend vineyards and a woman trudges along a
path winding through the blossoming orchard. The château and its
famous terraces are visible in the distance at the left.

37
Alfred Sisley

Paris, 1839–Moret-sur-Loing, 1899
View of Saint-Mammès, 1881
oil on canvas
21½ x 29⅛ in (54 x 74 cm)
Inscribed: *Sisley*
The Walters Art Gallery, 37.355

Purchased by Henry Walters, 1909

By 1880, the impressionists were beginning to pursue individual
courses. It was probably financial considerations that led to
Sisley's decision to leave the suburbs west of Paris, since dubbed
as "the cradle of Impressionism," and to return to the Forest of
Fontainebleau where he had begun to paint directly from nature.
He settled in the picturesque region around the town of Moret-
sur-Loing.

In 1881, he painted a sequence of views looking across the
water to the quai of Saint-Mammès, the barge-port at the conflu-
ence of the Loing and Seine rivers. He worked at different times
of the day and from slightly varying locations. Sisley abandoned
his earlier, lyrical technique and adopted a more vigorous,
expressive approach, applying his pigments in a richer impasto.
As in many of the artist's landscapes, the sky provides a key
component to the composition. In this view, clouds streak
across the sky reinforcing the diagonal recession established by
the river.

38

Pierre-Auguste Renoir

Limoges, 1841–Cagnes-sur-Mer, 1919

Child with a Hoop, ca. 1875

oil on canvas

24½ x 19¼ in (62.2 x 48.9 cm)

Inscribed: *Renoir*

The Baltimore Museum of Art

The Helen and Abram Eisenberg Collection, BMA 1976.55.8

Acquired by Mrs Abram Eisenberg, before 1935

Throughout Renoir's career, portraiture remained a dominant means of expression. Whether a commissioned work painted for a client or an informal likeness of a family member or friend, these images reveal essential elements of the sitter's life and personality.

Renoir's portraits of children are plentiful, especially after the birth of his first son, Pierre, in 1885, and the subsequent arrivals of brothers Jean, in 1894, and Claude, called Coco, in 1901. Here, a fair-haired child of two or three grasps a hoop, a toy observed in a number of Renoir's studies of children. Generally dated in the mid-1870s, the portrait is similar in style to the artist's *Portrait of Madame Charpentier and her Children*, from 1878 (New York, The Metropolitan Museum of Art). Although the identity of the young subject remains unknown, Renoir has presented a beguiling impression of childhood innocence and candor.

39

Pierre-Auguste Renoir

Limoges, 1841–Cagnes-sur-Mer, 1919

Washerwomen, ca. 1888

oil on canvas

22¼ x 18½ in (56.5 x 47 cm)

Inscribed: *Renoir*

The Baltimore Museum of Art

The Cone Collection, formed by Dr Claribel Cone and

Miss Etta Cone of Baltimore, Maryland, BMA 1950.282

Purchased by Etta Cone from Bernheim Jeune,
Paris, June 1928

In the autumn of 1888, Renoir was staying in Essoyes, the
hometown of his mistress of several years, Aline Charigot. In
a letter to Berthe Morisot and her husband, Eugène Manet,
he remarked: "I am in the process of being rusticated [here] in
Champagne in order to escape the expensive models in Paris.
I am doing some laundresses, or rather washerwomen, on the
banks of the river."

 Although relatively small in size, this painting presents a
complex, almost crowded, composition. Two women kneel at
the edge of the water washing laundry, which they have brought
in the basket in the right foreground. A third figure, thought to
be Aline, rolls up her sleeves and prepares to join them as she
speaks with a young child, identified as the artist's first son,
Pierre. The brushstroke is varied and animated, and the brilliant
colors throughout radiate the warmth of the sunny day. The
artist returned to the theme of washerwomen in 1912, painting
a series of varied compositions at Cagnes-sur-Mer, overlooking
the Mediterranean, where he spent the last years of his life.

 In the course of his career, Renoir painted women in a myriad
of guises, from the fashionable society matrons of his commissioned portraits, to actresses and bathers, to sympathetic like-
nesses of Aline Charigot, who became his wife in 1890.

 Etta Cone professed a great fondness for the *Washerwomen*.
In May 1946, three years before her death, she purchased a
watercolor study for it (BMA 1950.283).

40

Pierre-Auguste Renoir

Limoges, 1841–Cagnes-sur-Mer, 1919
Bouquet of Roses, ca. 1909
oil on canvas
21⅝ x 18⅛ in (54.9 x 46 cm)
Inscribed: *Renoir*
The Baltimore Museum of Art
The Cone Collection, formed by Dr Claribel Cone and
Miss Etta Cone of Baltimore, Maryland, BMA 1950.286

Purchased by Claribel Cone from Paul Vallotton,
Lausanne, August 1926

The Cone Collection includes a number of still lifes painted
mainly by artists who were contemporaries of the sisters. At
the same time as she purchased this work from Paul Vallotton,
Claribel also acquired a still life, *Roses and Black Cup*, 1918
(BMA 1950. 373), by his brother, the painter Félix.

   During the Second Empire, still life painting enjoyed a revival
and, at one time or another, virtually all of the impressionists
explored the genre. Renoir's initial employment as a decorator
of porcelain undoubtedly accounted for his sustained interest
in the subject. In addition to painting pure still life, he would
occasionally include an arrangement of flowers as a decorative
element in a larger composition, a practice also employed by his
impressionist colleagues. In 1867, Renoir presided over Frédéric
Bazille and Claude Monet as they executed their respective
interpretations of a grouping of dead birds, and recorded an
image of Bazille at his easel as he worked on his version
(*Frédéric Bazille Painting "The Heron,"* 1867, Paris, Musée
d'Orsay). Two years later, both Renoir and Monet would paint
still lifes from the same tabletop grouping of fruit and flowers.

   In this work, Renoir has recorded a sumptuous
arrangement of roses in full bloom. Dated about 1909, after the
artist had settled at Cagnes-sur-Mer, it speaks of his response to
color, his expressive handling of pigment and, above all, to his
pleasure in the varied manifestations of nature.

41

Pierre-Cécile Puvis de Chavannes

Lyon, 1824–Paris, 1898
Hope, 1872
oil on canvas
40³/₈ x 50⁷/₈ in (102.5 x 129.5 cm)
Inscribed: *1872 P. Puvis de Chavannes*
The Walters Art Gallery, 37.156

Purchased by Henry Walters, 1902

A visit to Italy in 1847 prompted Puvis de Chavannes to pursue a
career as an artist. He was essentially self-taught and developed
an independent style characterized by schematized compositions,
simplified planes of recession and muted colors. His approach
lent itself to mural painting, an art form that he reinvigorated
and for which he is chiefly remembered. Puvis' murals can be
seen in the Pantheon and the Hôtel de Ville in Paris, in buildings
in Amiens, Marseilles, Lyons and Poitiers as well as in the United
States in the Boston Public Library. He also produced a number
of easel paintings, which he usually sold through Paul Durand-
Ruel, the dealer remembered for his early recognition of the
impressionists.

   Hope is one of his three canvases resulting from the
calamities of the Franco-Prussian War of 1870/1, the others
being *The Balloon* and *The Carrier Pigeon* (both Paris, Musée
d'Orsay). Personifying the regeneration of France after defeat,
Hope is represented by a young girl clad in white, seated on a
masonry ledge amidst blossoming spring flowers. In her outstretched hand she holds a twig of oak. Discernible in the background are grave markers and the shattered ruins of buildings.
Puvis derived this imagery from a representation of "Good
Government" by the fourteenth-century artist Ambrogio
Lorenzetti, in the Palazzo Pubblico, Siena. A smaller version
of this composition differs in a number of details, but most
obviously in the rendering of the girl nude, seated on a white
drapery (Paris, Musée d'Orsay).

42

Georges-Pierre Seurat
Paris, 1859–Paris, 1891
Preparatory sketch for the painting
La Grève du Bas-Butin, Honfleur, 1886
oil on wood panel
6¾ x 10¼ in (17.2 x 26.1 cm)
The Baltimore Museum of Art
Bequest of Saidie A. May, BMA 1951.357

Purchased by Saidie A. May from Bernheim Jeune, Paris, 1925

In 1886, the year in which he exhibited *A Sunday Afternoon on the Island of the Grande-Jatte*, 1884/6 (The Art Institute of Chicago) and other innovative pointillist works at the Eighth Impressionist Exhibition, Seurat spent July and August at Honfleur on the coast of Normandy. He had produced his first group of marines the previous summer at Grandcamp, near Bayeux, and would return regularly to other Channel coast sites until his death in 1891. The seascapes that he painted during these campaigns are central to his œuvre, and the numerous preliminary studies he generated for finished works reveal his explorations of color theory and innovative pointillist technique.

Seurat's sojourn at Honfleur resulted in several finished canvases. This small panel is a preparatory sketch for *La Grève du Bas-Butin*, 1886 (Tournai, Musée des Beaux-Arts). Typically, touches of paint have been applied to a deep, warm-toned ground that remains visible, especially in the water and on the beach in the right foreground. Variations in the density of brushstroke serve to define specific passages. Slight differences in composition are apparent between this study and the final version, which also presents a somewhat more expansive view of the site. A critic writing about the artist's seascapes shown at the 1886 impressionist exhibition enthused: ". . . there is a vibration of light, a richness of color . . . a sweet and poetic harmony, an inexpressibly milky flowered quality that voluptuously caresses the retina."

43

Norbert Goeneutte

Paris, 1854–Auvers-sur-Oise, 1894

View of St Lazare Railway Station, Paris

(The Pont de l'Europe), 1887

oil on canvas

18³/₈ x 21⁷/₈ in (46.7 x 53.6 cm)

Inscribed: *Norbert Goeneutte Paris 18[8]7*

The Baltimore Museum of Art

George A. Lucas Collection, BMA 1996.45.118

Purchased by George Lucas from the artist, March 1888

A printmaker as well as a painter, Goeneutte was acquainted with several of the impressionists but never participated in their group exhibitions, preferring instead the official salons. Although he also painted portraits and landscapes, he specialized in views of modern Paris that record the everyday lives of both the working classes and of the fashionable Parisians.

In February 1887, he rented a third-floor studio on the rue de Rome that provided him with a panoramic view of the Pont de l'Europe and the Gare St Lazare, and, beyond, the cityscape of Paris. The bridge, completed in 1868, replaced antiquated tunnels that could no longer accommodate the increased traffic in the vicinity of the busy railroad station. Its massive stone pillars and distinctive iron girders symbolized Baron Haussmann's ongoing transformation of the city and were elements depicted by a number of Goeneutte's contemporaries, including Jean Béraud and Gustave Caillebotte. However, it is Claude Monet's series of views of the bridge and the station painted in the late 1870s that seem most closely associated with this composition.

Although Goeneutte had exhibited a pastel of the Pont de l'Europe at the 1884 Salon, he began to focus his efforts on the site following his move to the rue de Rome studio. This view looks down on the impressive bridge that spans the numerous train tracks leading to the station. Billowing clouds of steam rising from engines recall Monet's treatment of the subject. Beyond, on the horizon, Charles Garnier's new Opera House, opened in 1875, dwarfs its surroundings. Goeneutte painted this vista at different times of day, and in his particular attention to the effects of light on its various elements, he allies himself with the impressionists.

44

Paul Cézanne

Aix-en-Provence, 1839–Aix-en-Provence, 1906

Mont Sainte-Victoire Seen from the Bibémus Quarry, ca. 1897

oil on canvas

25⅛ x 31½ in (63.8 x 80 cm)

The Baltimore Museum of Art

The Cone Collection, formed by Dr Claribel Cone and

Miss Etta Cone of Baltimore, Maryland, BMA 1950.196

Purchased by Claribel Cone from Bernheim Jeune, Paris, June 1925

In the early 1870s, Cézanne fell under the influence of Camille Pissarro, who was working at Pontoise, north of Paris. In the course of the decade, his subjective, somewhat ponderous approach gradually gave way to a manner characterized by more delicate surfaces, a lighter palette and varied tonal relationships. He also became increasingly interested in landscape, painting views in the impressionist manner at Auvers-sur-Oise near Pontoise, L'Estaque on the Mediterranean coast and at his family's estate, La Jas de Bouffan, near Aix.

Cézanne began his explorations of Mont Sainte-Victoire, east of Aix, in the early 1880s with a series of graphic studies and oils that depict the mountain rising above the immense valley of the Arc River. The artist returned to the site once again in the mid-1890s, choosing a different vantage point, the deserted Bibémus quarry on the road leading to the town of Le Tholonet in the eastern environs of Aix. Clearly fascinated by the terrain of the locale, he produced works that record the complex rock formations. This landscape, which shows the quarry in the foreground and the distinctive silhouette of Mont Sainte-Victoire behind it, was probably painted during this period.

Cézanne defines the view with a masterful assortment of brush-strokes. Loosely painted trees in the foreground give way to patches of ochre pigment, their geometric forms and coloration reminiscent of the architecture of the region, shown in other views. Finally, planes of pale blues and grays, some arranged in arched bands, define the distinctive summit profiled against the sky. Of all the artist's Mont Sainte-Victoire landscapes, this is among the least expansive, the quarry appearing to abut the very base of the imposing peak.

During the last four years of his life, Cézanne returned to the mountain for the last time, painting a series of views from the hills near his studio at Les Lauves above Aix. Generally dark in tonality and vigorously executed, they represent his final, noble vision of the motif that had occupied him on and off throughout much of his career.

45

Vincent van Gogh

Zundert, Holland, 1853–Auvers-sur-Oise, 1890

A Pair of Boots (Les Souliers), 1887

oil on canvas

13 x 16⅛ in (33 x 40.9 cm)

Inscribed: *Vincent 87*

The Baltimore Museum of Art

The Cone Collection, formed by Dr Claribel Cone and

Miss Etta Cone of Baltimore, Maryland, BMA 1950.302

Purchased by Claribel Cone from Paul Vallotton,
Lausanne, September 1927

After attempting to pursue a variety of professions, including those of clergyman and art dealer, Van Gogh heeded his brother Theo's advice to become an artist. In early 1886, he arrived in Paris where he encountered the work of the impressionists and post-impressionists, and shortly thereafter abandoned the dark palette that had marked his earlier works.

During a two-year stay in Paris, he produced over one hundred paintings, which ranged in subject from landscapes to portraits and self-portraits, figure studies and still lifes. Within the latter genre are floral pieces, arrangements of books and various fruits and a series of remarkably expressive representations of workingmen's boots. According to a fellow painter, these were not Van Gogh's, but rather he had purchased them at the flea market and worn them until they had achieved the appropriate measure of wear.

In this poignant image, the boots have been carefully arranged on blue fabric. A pale brown passage in the background suggests a space beyond. Shoelaces from the boot on the right fall forward in an arabesque pattern. Although still somewhat dark in tonality, the painting demonstrates Van Gogh's transition toward the use of lighter colors, which reached fruition following his move to Arles in February 1888.

Writing to her sister, Etta, from Lausanne in August 1927, Claribel Cone expressed some reservation about the recently purchased still life: "I am not so pleased with my Van Gogh—it is so unlike his *better* (more forceful, more mad style perhaps) style. And the pair of shoes will not grace my livingroom with beauty—however—it is a Van Gogh—almost-certainly—Mr V. [Vallotton] says *sans doutes* . . ."

46

Vincent van Gogh

Zundert, Holland, 1853–Auvers-sur-Oise, 1890

Landscape with Figures, 1889

oil on canvas

19⅝ x 25¾ in (49.9 x 65.4 cm)

The Baltimore Museum of Art

The Cone Collection, formed by Dr Claribel Cone and

Miss Etta Cone of Baltimore, Maryland, BMA 1950.302

Purchased by Etta Cone from Galerie Rosengart,
Lucerne, August 1934

Like Millet, whom he greatly admired, Van Gogh often painted
landscapes that depict peasants in the fields and gardens that
they cultivated. Here, small figures working on the sloping hill-
side are all but lost in the forceful, rhythmic brushstrokes that
define the tracts of land. A woman at the right seems strangely
out of place in the setting, almost an afterthought in the
composition. A date of 1889 is generally assigned to this work;
however, the tall stand of trees with their elongated trunks and
dark foliage clustered at the top is more reminiscent of the
country-side at Auvers-sur-Oise, near Paris, where the artist
spent the last months of his life in 1890.

47

Paul Gauguin

Paris, 1848–Atuona, Marquesas Islands, 1903

Vahine no te vi (Woman of the Mango), 1892

oil on canvas

28⅝ x 17½ in (72.7 x 44.5 cm)

Inscribed: *Vahine no te vi/P Gauguin–92*

The Baltimore Museum of Art

The Cone Collection, formed by Dr Claribel Cone and

Miss Etta Cone of Baltimore, Maryland, BMA 1950.213

Purchased by Etta Cone from Galerie Rosengart,

Lucerne, August 1937

(American tour)

Following the stockmarket crash of 1882, Gauguin left the world
of finance to devote himself to painting, a pursuit that had co-
existed with his activities in business. Although he exhibited with
the impressionists in five of their eight group shows, he would
gradually abandon the movement, claiming that its adherents
"heed only the eye and neglect the mysterious centers of thought."
During the late 1880s and early 1890s, he developed a highly
personal style marked by simplified form, decorative line and
flat, often arbitrary, use of expressive color. Contributing to these
innovations were his contacts at Pont Aven with Emile Bernard,
the chief exponent of Cloisonnism, and Vincent van Gogh, whom
he visited at Arles in 1888.

In his quest for a utopian lifestyle from which to draw inspiration, Gauguin set out for Tahiti in 1891. His account of the two-
year sojourn, *Noa–Noa*, describes the circumstances under which
he took a young native girl Tehamana as his wife. She was his
model in several works, including this portrait from 1892. A
highly decorative composition with vivid color and a complex
arrangement of forms, it presents the figure filling nearly the
entire canvas. At a Paris sale organized by the artist in 1895,
prior to his final departure for Tahiti, it was purchased by Edgar
Degas, an enthusiastic admirer, for his personal collection.

48

Paul Gauguin

Paris, 1848–Atuona, Marquesas Islands, 1903

Upaupa Schneklud (The Player Schneklud), 1894

oil on canvas

36½ x 28⅞ in (92.5 x 73.5 cm)

Inscribed: *Upaupa SCHNEKLUD/P Gauguin/94*

The Baltimore Museum of Art

Given by Hilda K. Blaustein, in Memory of her late Husband,

Jacob Blaustein, BMA 1979.163

Purchased by Jacob Blaustein at Parke-Bernet Galleries Inc.,

New York, October 1940

(Royal Academy of Arts)

Painted during his two-year hiatus in France from 1893 to 1895,
Gauguin's portrait of his friend and cellist Frédéric-Guillaume
Schneklud presents an image as compelling as that in *Vahine
no te vi*. An abstract setting is the background for the musician,
who listens intently as he plays. It has been observed that
Schneklud and Gauguin bore a striking resemblance to one
another, suggesting that this portrait is a synthesis of artist and
sitter. The painting also alludes to Gauguin's two worlds of
France and the South Seas, through the introduction of the
word "Upaupa" inscribed in the upper left, a reference to a
sensual rhythmic Tahitian dance.

49

Odilon Redon
Bordeaux, 1840–Paris, 1916
Peonies, ca. 1900/5
oil on canvas
20⅛ x 17¾ in (51.1 x 45.1 cm)
The Baltimore Museum of Art
The Cone Collection, formed by Dr Claribel Cone and
Miss Etta Cone of Baltimore, Maryland, BMA 1950.281

Purchased by Claribel Cone from Paul Vallotton,
Lausanne, September 1927

It has been said that Redon was one of the most mysterious figures in the history of late nineteenth- and early twentieth-century French art. Following a brief period of study in Paris with Jean-Léon Gérôme, Redon returned to Bordeaux where he developed an admiration for the work of Delacroix, Corot and the symbolist Gustave Moreau. He was, however, most captivated by the prints of Rodolphe Bresdin, who created fantastic, sometimes macabre, images inspired by the graphics of Dürer and Rembrandt.

From 1870 to 1890, Redon worked almost exclusively in black and white. A series of charcoal drawings called *Noirs*, evoking his melancholy world, preceded a period devoted to lithography, which would occupy him through the 1880s and 1890s. Settling in Paris, he became part of its rich intellectual life. His mystical, often decadent, imagery appealed in particular to such symbolist writers as Stéphane Mallarmé and Joris Karl Huysmans.

Around 1890, Redon's art underwent a major change with the introduction of pure, opulent color. Although he continued to present images drawn from his complex inner world, he turned to new subject matter, notably flowers. Working in both pastel and oil, he carefully recorded a wide range of species with almost scientific accuracy. For the most part, the flowers are arranged in vases that are presented in completely neutral surroundings. Here, the artist has painted red peonies and other small brightly colored blooms. There is only the suggestion of a tabletop, and the still life seems suspended within its own intimate space.

50

Henri Rousseau

Laval, 1844–Paris, 1910

*View of the Quai d'Ivry near the Port à l'Anglais, Seine
(Family Fishing)*, 1900

oil on canvas

9½ x 13 in (24.1 x 33 cm)

Inscribed: *H. Rousseau/1900*

The Baltimore Museum of Art

The Cone Collection, formed by Dr Claribel Cone and
Miss Etta Cone of Baltimore, Maryland, BMA 1950.294

Purchased by Etta Cone from Galerie Rosengart,
Lucerne, August 1936

Rousseau, an ex-soldier and minor customs official, the
occupation from which his nickname, "Le Douanier," derives,
retired in 1893 to devote himself to art. Self-taught, he is known
to have copied paintings in the Louvre. Early in his artistic
career, he developed a distinctive style, which he altered very
little thereafter. The naïve directness of his work, his particular
range of subjects and his innate sense of design made him the
most admired of the primitive artists.

Among Rousseau's supporters were several of the younger,
progressive artists and writers working in Paris at the turn of
the century. In 1908, Picasso, who had purchased one of his
paintings, which he kept until his death, presided over a
legendary banquet organized in Rousseau's honor. The guests
included Apollinaire, Marie Laurencin, Georges Braque and
others. Robert Delaunay, Vassily Kandinsky and the Russian
collector Sergei Shchukin were also early devotees.

When painting the Paris landscape, Rousseau was often
attracted to its more commonplace aspects. Factories, bridges
and river quays in the city and its environs appear with regularity
in his work, especially toward the end of his life. A man quietly
fishing on the bank of a river was a subject often favored by the
artist. Here, the fisherman is accompanied by his wife and infant.
A sailboat is moored nearby and simple buildings dot the opposite bank. Typically, the figures are small and seem dwarfed by
the setting and an expansive sky.

51

Pierre Bonnard

Fontenay-aux-Roses, near Paris, 1867–Le Cannet, 1947
Woman with Basket of Fruit, 1915/18
oil on canvas
27 x 15½ in (68.6 x 39.4 cm)
Inscribed: *Bonnard*
The Baltimore Museum of Art
The Cone Collection, Bequest of Frederic W. Cone, BMA 1950.190

In his formative years, Bonnard was a member of the Nabis (Hebrew for "prophets"), a group of painters who adopted Paul Gauguin's expressive use of color and rhythmical patterns and were also inspired by Japanese wood-block prints that they encountered at a large exhibition at the École des Beaux-Arts in 1890. Early in his career, he also became involved in printmaking, producing posters and illustrations for various publications, notably the avant-garde *Revue Blanche*. Although Fauvism and Cubism were evolving in the early years of the twentieth century, he remained essentially independent, developing his own unique approach toward the use of color and composition.

Bonnard painted landscapes and still lifes throughout his career, but it is in his works incorporating figures that he was often the most inventive. While portraits and nude studies appear regularly, he also combined figures with other elements, frequently placing them in domestic settings. In this work, a woman, resting her head in her hand, shares the tabletop with a large basket of fruit. The background only suggests the interior space. The brown dog in the immediate foreground appears in a number of works from the period and has been identified as Ubu, a pet belonging to Marthe Bonnard, the artist's wife. The vertical format favored by the artist in many of his works is emphasized by the placement of the woman above and the dog's head below the fruit in the center. Dramatic elements in the composition are the viewpoint, which looks down onto the table, and the cropping at the top of the image, both features reminiscent of Japanese art.

This painting belonged to Frederic W. Cone (1878–1944), youngest of the Cone siblings, and was part of the Cone bequest, which came to the Museum in 1950.

52

Pablo Picasso

Malaga, Spain, 1881–Mougins, 1973

Woman with Bangs, 1902

oil on canvas

23⅝ x 19¼ in (60 x 48.9 cm)

Inscribed: *Picasso*

The Baltimore Museum of Art

The Cone Collection, formed by Dr Claribel Cone and

Miss Etta Cone of Baltimore, Maryland, BMA 1950.268

Purchased by Etta Cone from Gertrude Stein, Paris, 1929/30

In the early years of the twentieth century, a youthful Picasso traveled regularly between Spain and Paris, where he was influenced by Art Nouveau and the *fin-de-siècle* aesthetic of such artists as Toulouse-Lautrec and Edvard Munch. He also developed an appreciation for the work of El Greco. The suicide of a fellow painter, Carles Casagemas, in February 1901, had a profound effect on Picasso, and it has been said that the tragic event precipitated the adoption of a predominately somber blue palette during the years 1901/4.

Gertrude Stein, whom Picasso met in Paris in 1905, offered her own explanation of his Blue Period:

> He went back again to Spain [from Paris] in 1902 and the painting known as his blue period was the result of that return. The sadness of Spain and the monotony of the Spanish coloring, after the time he spent in Paris, struck him forcibly upon his return there. . . . Spain . . . is not like other southern countries, it is not colorful . . . . There is no red or green. . . . [Spain] is oriental, women there wear black more often than colors . . . the sky is blue almost black. . . . (Gertrude Stein, *Picasso*, 1938).

Throughout the autumn of 1901, spent in Paris, and into the following year, when he lived for several months in Barcelona, the artist limited his pigments to predominately blue tones. With the somber palette came imagery focusing on the miseries of poverty, prostitution and psychological depression.

Woman with Bangs typifies Picasso's production in this period. A dark-haired woman with downcast, unfocused eyes is lost in reverie. The simplicity of her surroundings and attire give emphasis to her face, with its expression of profound dejection. An uneasiness prevails, the result of the placement of the figure slightly off center.

With his permanent return to France in 1904, Picasso's colors gradually changed, evolving into the delicate pink and flesh tones of his Rose Period, which prevailed during the next two years.

53

Pablo Picasso

Malaga, Spain, 1881–Mougins, 1973

Mother and Child, 1922

oil on canvas

$39^{3}/_{8}$ x $31^{7}/_{8}$ in (100 x 81 cm)

Inscribed: *Picasso/22*

The Baltimore Museum of Art

The Cone Collection, formed by Dr Claribel Cone and

Miss Etta Cone of Baltimore, Maryland, BMA 1950.279

Purchased by Etta Cone from Galerie Rosengart,
Lucerne, August 1939

Concurrent with his explorations of Cubism in the early 1920s, Picasso developed a mode of expression rooted in Classicism. Monumental nudes and draped figures are presented with heavy, almost sculptural, bodies. Around 1922, he abandoned these ponderous images and turned to a more lyrical, delicate neoclassical style, which he employed in both paintings and drawings.

In 1921, the artist's wife, Olga, a dancer whom he had met in Rome four years earlier while designing stage sets for Serge Diaghilev's Ballets Russes, gave birth to a son, Paulo. Over the next several years, the theme of maternity appeared frequently in his work. This painting, which is more a drawing in oil on canvas, captures a tender moment between mother and child with an economy of line and only a hint of restrained color. Both in composition and in theme, the work is reminiscent of Renaissance paintings of the Madonna.

Some question has been raised regarding the identity of the woman in this work and in a related, nearly identical, version (formerly Collection of Pamela Harriman). Long thought to be portraits of Olga and Paulo, it has been suggested that the woman is in fact Sara Murphy, wife of the American expatriate painter Gerald Murphy. Picasso was infatuated with her in the early 1920s, and she is thought to have been the subject of nearly 40 paintings and more than 200 drawings.

54

Marie Laurencin

Paris, 1883–Paris, 1956

Group of Artists, 1908

oil on canvas

24¾ x 31⅛ in (62.9 x 79.1 cm)

Inscribed: *Marie Laurencin/1908*

The Baltimore Museum of Art

The Cone Collection, formed by Dr Claribel Cone and

Miss Etta Cone of Baltimore, Maryland, BMA 1950.215

Purchased by Claribel Cone from Gertrude Stein, Paris, June 1925

Best remembered for her images of large-eyed young women
rendered in a distinctly feminine manner, Laurencin was also
a prolific printmaker and stage designer. In 1907, she met
Picasso and, through him, the poet Guillaume Apollinaire,
with whom she had a lengthy and tempestuous love affair.
Her early years were spent in the company of such avant-garde
artists and writers as Georges Braque, Juan Gris and Gertrude
and Leo Stein.

The flat areas of bold color, simplified form and lack of depth
in this work, all speak to Laurencin's early artistic associations.
The central figure in the group is Apollinaire, seated holding an
open book befitting his literary pursuits. The artist herself, with
a portion of her face in shadow, stands behind him. Next to her
is Picasso, presented in profile, accompanied by his dog, Frika.
His dark hair and his eye, dramatically outlined, give a marked
intensity to his characterization. The fourth figure on the right,
Picasso's mistress at the time, Fernande Olivier, seems bemused,
her image somewhat compromised by the elaborate floral
arrangement above her head.

According to Gertrude Stein, who bought the painting from
Laurencin, it was the first work sold by the artist.

55

Henri Matisse

Le Cateau-Cambrésis [now Le Cateau], Picardy, 1869–Nice, 1954
Interior, Flowers and Parakeets, 1924
oil on canvas
46 x 28⅝ in (116.9 x 72.7 cm)
Inscribed: *Henri-Matisse*
The Baltimore Museum of Art
The Cone Collection, formed by Dr Claribel Cone and
Miss Etta Cone of Baltimore, Maryland, BMA 1950.252

Purchased by Etta Cone from Pierre Matisse, Paris, July 1925
(Royal Academy of Arts)

Among the most significant influences on Matisse during his
formative years were the teachings of the colorist Gustave Moreau
at the École des Beaux-Arts, and the works of the impressionists
and post-impressionists, in particular the figure studies and
compositions of Paul Cézanne. In the early years of the twentieth
century, he became increasingly involved with a group of avant-
garde artists, including André Derain and Maurice de Vlaminck,
who were intent on using bright color in an expressive, sponta-
neous manner. When they exhibited together at the Salon
d'Automne in October 1905, they were given the derisive name,
the Fauves (beasts), with Matisse acknowledged as their leader.

Throughout the following decade, Matisse continued to explore
the use of line and vibrant color, often arranged in patterns. In
some compositions, which border on abstraction, he also acknowledged the cubist movement and its emphasis on fragmentation
and geometric shape. Visits to Algeria (1906), the great Islamic
exhibition in Munich (1910) and subsequent travels to Moorish
Spain (1911) and Morocco (1912/13) also exerted a significant
influence on his work, which became richer and more decorative.

In the autumn of 1917, Matisse settled in Nice, where he
would reside for the rest of his life, returning to Paris only in the
summer months to avoid the heat of the south. Although many
of his Nice paintings include figures often seductively dressed,
others focus on interior views that combine such elements as
still lifes, exotic wall coverings and patterned floors, and frequently
include a window with a glimpse of buildings or the sea beyond.

This work shows the interior of the artist's apartment on the
Place Charles-Félix in Nice, which he occupied from 1921 to 1938.
A flower-filled vase and a bird-cage with two parakeets sit on the
table, partially covered with a brightly colored cloth.

56

Henri Matisse

Le Cateau-Cambrésis [now Le Cateau], Picardy, 1869–Nice, 1954

Odalisque with Green Sash, 1927

oil on canvas

20 x 25½ in (50.8 x 64.8 cm)

Inscribed: *Henri-Matisse*

The Baltimore Museum of Art

The Cone Collection, formed by Dr Claribel Cone and

Miss Etta Cone of Baltimore, Maryland, BMA 1950.253

Purchased by Etta Cone from Galerie Rosengart,

Lucerne, August 1937

(Royal Academy of Arts)

In an article entitled "Notes of a Painter," written in 1908, Matisse explained: "What interests me most is neither still life nor landscape but the human figure. It is through it that I best succeed in expressing the nearly religious feeling that I have towards life." For the most part, Matisse's subjects were women, and he employed a succession of models. On occasion, his wife, Amélie, and daughter, Marguerite, also posed for him.

During his early years in Nice, the artist engaged a young woman named Henriette Darricarrère, who would be his primary model from 1920 to 1927. Born in 1901, she lived with her family not far from Matisse's Place Charles-Félix apartment. A student of music and ballet, she was especially adept at portraying the various roles envisioned by the artist for the figures in his compositions. Whether posing nude in an interior, standing on a balcony overlooking the Mediterranean or simply reading at a table, she seemed the perfect model.

Henriette's sculpturesque body and dark coloring were especially suited to Matisse's studies of odalisques. In this work, she reclines langorously against a richly patterned background. Semi-nude, her only clothes are the pantaloons, edged with a green sash, which are loosely arranged around her hips. The shiny samovar and the table in the background are elements observed in other compositions of the period. Henriette would eventually marry, leaving Matisse to search for other models capable of conveying his evolving artistic vision.

57

Henri Matisse

Le Cateau-Cambrésis [now Le Cateau], Picardy, 1869–Nice, 1954

Purple Robe and Anemones, 1937

oil on canvas

28$^3/_4$ x 23$^3/_4$ in (73.1 x 60.3 cm)

Inscribed: *Henri Matisse 37*

The Baltimore Museum of Art

The Cone Collection, formed by Dr Claribel Cone and
Miss Etta Cone of Baltimore, Maryland, BMA 1950.261

Purchased by Etta Cone from Paul Rosenberg, Paris, August 1937

During the late 1930s, Matisse embarked on a series of decorative paintings portraying models in interior settings. In their vibrant tones and juxtaposition of patterns and contours, these works achieve a perfect fusion of line and color.

The coloring and features of the young woman in this composition suggest that she is Lydia Delectorskaya, who had been the artist's studio assistant earlier in the decade when he was involved in the mural decorations for the Barnes Foundation at Merion Station, Pennsylvania. In 1935, Lydia began to pose for Matisse, and she is the model seen in such celebrated works as *Large Reclining Nude (The Pink Nude)*, 1935 (The Baltimore Museum of Art) and *Woman in Blue*, 1937 (Philadelphia Museum of Art). In the latter, she wears an equally elaborate costume, and is also seated frontally with one hand raised to her head and the other resting in her lap. In another version of the Baltimore picture, in which the interior decor is somewhat different, the figure dressed in the purple robe has darker hair and a rather dissimilar appearance, suggesting that Matisse employed a model other than Lydia for the work (*Woman in a Purple Robe with Ranunculi*, 1937, The Museum of Fine Arts, Houston).

NOTES TO ESSAY

1 Lillian B. Miller, *Patrons and Patriotism: The Encouragement of the Fine Arts in the United States, 1790–1860*, Chicago, Illinois, 1966, p. 130.

2 Jérome Bonaparte, Jr, was born in Camberwell in England in 1805 and died in Baltimore in 1870. His sons included Jérome Napoleon Bonaparte (1830–79) and Charles Joseph Bonaparte (1851–1920).

3 Other short-lived cultural institutions included the Baltimore Athenaeum, which opened in 1824 and closed in the 1830s; The Maryland Academy of the Fine Arts (active in 1838); and the Maryland Art Association (about 1847). The Maryland Historical Society, which remains active today, was founded in 1844 and began to organize art exhibitions in 1847. After 1879, the Peabody Institute briefly rivaled the Maryland Historical Society as an art gallery.

4 Gilmor MS, "Memorandums made in a Tour of the Eastern States in the Year 1797," reprinted in *Bulletin of the Boston Public Library*, II: I (April 1892): pp. 75–6.

5 "List of Paintings belonging to the Estate of Dr Edmondson . . . January 1859," Archives of the Maryland Historical Society (MS 2008).

6 *Catalogue of Valuable Paintings, the entire collection of Mr Granville Sharp Oldfield at his residence, Mount Vernon Place, May 15 and following*, Carroll Hall, Baltimore, 1855.

7 The primary source for information on Lucas and his activities is *The Diary of George A. Lucas: An American Art Agent in Paris, 1857–1909*, transcribed and with an introduction by Lilian M. C. Randall, 2 vols, Princeton, New Jersey, Princeton University Press, 1979.

8 Gertrude Rosenthal, "The Collector and his Collection," in *The George A. Lucas Collection, an exhibition at The Baltimore Museum of Art*, Baltimore, 1965, p. 14. Eventually, in August 1886, the artist painted a portrait of Lucas as an oil sketch, which the subject presented to Henry Walters in 1908.

9 Elizabeth R. Pennell and Joseph Pennell, *The Whistler Journal*, Philadelphia, Pennsylvania, J. B. Lippincott & Co., 1921, p. 55.

10 In 1996, with the assistance of state and private monies, the George A. Lucas Collection, with the exception of five works of art acquired by the Walters Art Gallery, was purchased by The Baltimore Museum of Art, where it had been on extended loan since 1933.

11 For William T. Walters, see William R. Johnston, *William and Henry Walters: The Reticent Collectors*, Baltimore, Maryland, Johns Hopkins University Press, 1999.

12 M. Reizenstein, "The Walters Art Gallery," *New England Magazine*, n.s. 12 (July 1895), p. 558.

13 *Dead Caesar (César mort)*, 1859. Sold by The Corcoran Gallery of Art. Washington, D.C., 1951.

14 George Peabody (1795–1869) resided in Baltimore from 1815 to 1837 and subsequently founded the Peabody Institute in this city. Johns Hopkins (1795–1873) provided for the founding of the Johns Hopkins University and the Johns Hopkins Hospital; and Baltimore's third great philanthropist, Enoch Pratt (1808–96), established the Enoch Pratt Free Library System.

15 John R. Tait, "Art in Baltimore," *Lippincott's Magazine*, Philadelphia, November 1883, p. 531. He cites among the city's artists, Richard Caton Woodville, William R. [sic] Rinehart and, ironically, James Abbott McNeill Whistler, who sometimes professed to be a Baltimorean.

16 Edward Strahan (Earl Shinn), *The Art Treasures of America*, Philadelphia, n.d. (ca. 1879–80), 3 vols, 3: p. 75.

17 *Catalogue of Paintings and Other Works of Art belonging to J. Stricker Jenkins, No. 176 N. Charles Street*, Baltimore, 1870.

18 Edward King, "The Liverpool of America," *Scribner's Monthly, an Illustrated Magazine for the People*, 9:6 (April 1875), p. 694.

19 Margie H. Luckett, *Maryland Women*, Baltimore, Maryland, King Brothers Inc., 1931, pp. 215–18.

20 For Jacob Epstein, see Lester S. Levy, *Jacob Epstein*, Baltimore, Maryland, 1978, and *The Jacob Epstein Collection*, privately printed by Jacob Epstein, Baltimore, 1939.

21 *Baltimore Sun*, 28 December 1945, pp. 8 and 22.

22 See typescript of remarks by Gerson Eisenberg on the occasion of the dedication of the Eisenberg Collection at The Baltimore Museum of Art, 1967 (Walters Art Gallery Archives). For the American tour of *The Angelus*, see Julia M. Cartwright, *Jean François Millet, His Life and Letters*, London and New York, The MacMillan Co., 1902, pp. 365–70.

23 For Henry Walters, see W. R. Johnston, 1999, *op. cit.*

24 The most comprehensive source for the Cone sisters and the formation of their collection is: Brenda Richardson, *Dr Claribel and Miss Etta, The Cone Collection of The Baltimore Museum of Art*, The Baltimore Museum of Art, Baltimore, Maryland, 1985. Of particular relevance is the annotated chronology of their purchases, which is the basis for the discussion herein.

25 Letter dated 22 July 1933, Nice, quoted in Richardson, 1985, *op. cit.*

26 *The Cone Collection of Baltimore, Maryland: Catalogue of Paintings-Drawings-Sculpture of the Nineteenth and Twentieth Centuries*, with a Foreword by George Boas, Baltimore, Maryland, 1934, p. 12.

27 Richardson, 1985, *op. cit.*, p. 53.

28 For Saidie A. May, see "Saidie A. May Collection," exhibition catalogue, published as *The Baltimore Museum of Art Record*, 3:1, 1927.

INDEX

Mr and Mrs Donald P Kahn
Mr and Mrs Joseph Karaviotis
Mr and Mrs James Kirkman
Mr and Mrs Henry L R Kravis
The Kreitman Foundation
Mrs Thomas Kressner
Mr and Mrs Irvine Laidlaw
The Kirby Laing Foundation
Mrs Panagiotis Lemos
Mr George Lengvari
The Lady Lever of Manchester
Mr and Mrs John Lewis
Sir Sydney Lipworth QC and Lady
  Lipworth
Mr Jonathon E Lyons
Fiona Mactaggart
Sir John and Lady Mactaggart
Mr and Mrs Michael (RA) and José
  Manser
Mr and Mrs M Margulies
Marsh Christian Trust
R C Martin
Mrs Jack Maxwell
Sir Kit and Lady McMahon
The Mercers' Company
Lt Col L S Michael OBE
Nancy Miller Jong
Mr and Mrs Peter Morgan
Mr Thomas F Mosimann III
Mr Harry Moss
Jim Moyes
Mr and Mrs Carl Anton Muller
Paul and Alison Myners
John Nickson and Simon Rew
Mr Michael Palin
Lord and Lady Palumbo
Mrs Chrysanthy Pateras
Lynda Pearson
The Pennycress Trust
The P F Charitable Trust
Miss Karen Phillipps
Mr Godfrey Pilkington
George and Carolyn Pincus
Mr and Mrs William A Plapinger
The Quercus Trust
Barbara Rae RA
John and Anne Raisman
The Rayne Foundation
Mrs Jean Redman-Brown
Mr T H Reitman
Mr and Mrs Robert E Rhea
Sir John and Lady Riddell
Mr and Mrs John Ritblat
Mr John A Roberts FRIBA
Mr and Mrs Nicholas Rohatyn
Mr and Mrs Ian Rosenberg
Alastair and Sarah Ross Goobey
Mrs Coral Samuel CBE
Mr and Mrs Victor Sandelson
Mr Adrian Sassoon
Ms Pierrette Schlettwein
Dr Lewis Sevitt
The Cyril Shack Trust
The Countess of Shaftesbury
Mr and Mrs D M Shalit
Mrs Stella Shawzin
Mr and Mrs Clive Sherling
Mrs Lois Sieff OBE
Silhouette Eyewear
Mr and Mrs Richard Simmons
Mr Peter Simon
Mrs Roama Spears
James and Alyson Spooner
Mr and Mrs Nicholas Stanley
Mrs Jack Steinberg

Mr and Mrs David Stileman
Swan Trust
Mr and Mrs David Swift
Mr and The Hon Mrs Richard Szpiro
Sir Anthony and Lady Tennant
Eugene V and Clare E Thaw
  Charitable Trust
Mr and Mrs Julian Treger
Mrs Claire Vyner
The Walter Guinness Charitable Trust
John B Watton
Edna and Willard Weiss
Mr and Mrs Anthony Weldon
Mrs Gerald Westbury
Mrs Linda M Williams
Roger and Jennifer Wingate
Mr and Mrs Rainer Zietz
Mr and Mrs Michael Zilkha
*and others who wish to remain
anonymous*

BENJAMIN WEST GROUP DONORS
The Benjamin West Group was
founded in March 1998 for American
citizens living temporarily or
permanently in Britain. The group
takes its name from Benjamin West,
a founder Member of the Royal
Academy and the first American artist
to become an Academician who also
served as President from 1790 to 1805
and from 1806 to his death in 1820.
The Royal Academy is delighted to
thank the following members of the
group who have also generously
contributed donations of £1,000 and
more to support the conservation of
works touring the United States in the
exhibition *The Royal Academy in the
Age of Queen Victoria 1837–1901:
Paintings and Sculpture from the
Permanent Collection.*

PATRON
The Hon Raymond G H Seitz

CHAIRMAN
The Hon Barbara S Thomas

DONORS
Mr Paul Abecassis
Mrs Wendy Becker Payton
Bernadette J Berger
Mr and Mrs Charles Brocklebank
Mr and Mrs Paul Collins
Mrs Joan Curci
Miss Elizabeth Gage
Mr and Mrs John Gore
Mrs Robin Hambro
Lady Harvie-Watt
Mr and Mrs Peter Holstein
Mr Paul Josefowitz
Mr and Mrs Richard Kaufman
Mr and Mrs Philip Mengel
Mr and Mrs Donald Moore
Mr Neil Osborn and Ms Holly Smith
Sir William and Lady Purves
Mrs Robert Rose
Albert and Marjorie Scardino
Mrs Sylvia B Scheuer
Mr and Mrs Paul Shang
Barbara and Allen Thomas
Mr Fred M Vinton
*and others who wish to remain
anonymous*

AMERICAN ASSOCIATES OF
THE ROYAL ACADEMY TRUST

BENEFACTORS
American Express
Mrs Russell B Aitken
Chase Manhattan Bank
Mr Walter Fitch III
Mrs Henry Ford II
The Honorable Amalia L de Fortabat
Glaxo Wellcome
The Horace W Goldsmith Foundation
Mr and Mrs Lewis P Grinnan Jr
Mrs Henry J Heinz II
Mr and Mrs Donald Kahn
Mr and Mrs Jon B Lovelace
Mr and Mrs John L Marion
Mrs Jack C Massey
Mr and Mrs Michael Meehan II
Mr Charles J Meyers
Mrs Nancy B Negley
Mrs Arthur M Sackler
Mrs Louisa S Sarofim
The Starr Foundation
The Honorable John C Whitehead
Mr and Mrs Frederick B Whittemore
Mrs William W Wood Prince
*and others who wish to remain
anonymous*

SPONSORS
The Honorable and Mrs Walter H
  Annenberg
Mr and Mrs Samuel R Blount
Mrs Jan Cowles
Mrs Donald Findlay
Mr D Francis Finlay
Mr James Kemper
Ms Stephanie Krieger
Mrs Linda Noe Laine
Mrs Janice H Levin
Mr and Mrs Vernon Taylor Jr
Prince Charitable Trusts
Mrs Sylvia Scheuer
US Trust Company of New York
*and others who wish to remain
anonymous*

PATRONS
Mr and Mrs John W Annan
Mr and Mrs Robert J Arnold
Mr and Mrs Stephen D Bechtel Jr
Mrs Helen Benedict
Mr and Mrs James Benson
Mrs Bette Berry
Mr Donald A Best
Ms Jan Blaustein Scholes
Mr and Mrs Henry W Breyer III
Mrs Mildred C Brinn
Mrs Caroline Chapin
Mrs Helene Chiang
Mr William L Clark
Ms Dorothea F Darlington
Ms Anne S Davidson
Mrs Charles H Dyson
Mrs John W Embry
Lady Warwick Fairfax
Mrs A Barlow Ferguson
Mrs Robert Ferst
Mr Ralph A Fields
Mr Richard E Ford
Mr and Mrs Lawrence S Friedland
Mrs Roswell L Gilpatric
Mr and Mrs Ralph W Golby
Mrs Betty N Gordon

Mrs Melville Wakeman Hall
Mr and Mrs Gurnee F Hart
Mr and Mrs Gustave M Hauser
The Honorable Marife Hernandez
Mr Robert J Irwin
Ms Betty Wold Johnson and Mr
  Douglas Bushnell
Ms Barbara R Jordan
The Honorable and Mrs Eugene
  Johnston
Mr William W Karatz
Mr and Mrs Stephen M Kellen
Mr Gary A Kraut
Mrs Katherine K Lawrence
Mr and Mrs William M Lese
Dr and Mrs Peter Linden
Mrs John P McGrath
Mrs Mark Millard
Mr Achim Moeller
Mrs Robin Heller Moss
Mr Paul D Myers
Ms Diane A Nixon
Mr and Mrs Jeffrey Pettit
Mr Robert S Pirie
Dr and Mrs Meyer P Potamkin
The Honorable and Mrs Charles H Price II
Mrs Signe E Ruddock
Mrs Frances G Scaife
Mrs Frederick M Stafford
Mr and Mrs Robert L Sterling Jr
Mrs Kenneth Straus
Mr Arthur O Sulzberger and Ms Alison
  S Cowles
Mrs Frederick Supper
Mrs Royce Dean Tate
Mr and Mrs A Alfred Taubman
Ms Britt Tidelius
Mrs Susan E Van de Bovenkamp
Mrs Bruce E Wallis
Mrs Sara E White
Mrs Joseph R Wier
Mrs Mary Louise Whitmarsh
Mr Robert W Wilson
Mr and Mrs Kenneth Woodcock
*and others who wish to remain
anonymous*

FRIENDS OF THE
ROYAL ACADEMY

PATRON FRIENDS
Mrs Denise Adeane
Mr Paul Baines
Mr P F J Bennett
Mr and Mrs Sidney Corob
Mr Michael Godbee
Mrs M C Godwin
Mr David Ker
Mr Andrew D Law
Dr Abraham Marcus
Mr Thomas Mosimann
Mr and Mrs David Peacock
Mr and Mrs Derald H Ruttenberg
Mr Nigel J Stapleton
Mr Robin Symes
Mrs K L Troughton
Mrs Cynthia H Walton
Mrs Roger Waters
The Hon Mrs Simon Weinstock
Miss Elizabeth White
Mr David Wolfers
Mrs I Wolstenholme
*and others who wish to remain
anonymous*

SUPPORTING FRIENDS

Mr Richard B Allan
Mr Peter Allinson
Mr Ian Anstruther
Mr John R Asprey
Mrs Yvonne Barlow
Mr J M Bartos
Mrs Wendy Becker-Payton
Mrs Susan Besser
Mrs C W T Blackwell
Mr Christopher Boddington
Mr Peter Boizot MBE DL
Mrs J M Bracegirdle
Mr Cornelius Broere
Mrs Gertraud Brutsche
Mrs Anne Cadbury OBE JP DL
Mr W L Carey-Evans
Miss E M Cassin
Mr R A Cernis
Mrs Norma Chaplin
Mr S Chapman
Mr W J Chapman
Mr and Mrs John Cleese
Mrs Ruth Cohen
Mrs D H Costopoulos
Mr and Mrs Chris Cotton
Mrs Saeda H Dalloul
Mr John Denham
Miss N J Dhanani
The Marquess of Douro
Mr Kenneth Edwards
Mrs Nicholas Embiricos
Mr and Mrs John R Farmer
Mr Ian S Ferguson
Mrs R H Goddard
Mr Gavin Graham
Mrs Richard Grogan
Miss Julia Hazandras
Mr Malcolm P Herring
Mr R J Hoare
Mr Charles Howard
Mrs O Hudson
Mrs Manya Igel
Mr S Isern-Feliu
Mrs Jane Jason
Mr Harold Joels
Mr and Mrs S D Kahan
Mrs P Keely
Mr and Mrs J Kessler
Mr D H Killick
Mr N R Killick
Mr Peter W Kininmonth
Mrs Joan Lavender
Mr and Mrs David Leathers
Mr Owen Luder CBE PRIBA FRSA
Miss Julia MacRae
Mr Donald A Main
Ms Rebecca Marek
The Hon Simon Marks
Mrs Janet Marsh
Mr J B H Martin
Mrs Gillian M S McIntosh
Mr J Moores
Mrs A Morgan
Miss Kim Nicholson
Mrs E M Oppenheim Sandelson
Mr Brian Oury
Mrs J Pappworth
Mrs M C S Philip
Mrs Anne Phillips
Mr Ralph Picken
Mr William Plapinger
Mr Benjamin Pritchett-Brown
Mr Clive Richards
Mr F Peter Robinson

Mr D S Rocklin
Mrs A Rodman
Mr and Mrs O Roux
The Hon Sir Steven Runciman CH
Dr Susan Saga
Sir Robert and Lady Sainsbury
Mr G Salmanowitz
Mr Anthony Salz
Mr and Mrs Julian Schild
Dr I B Schulenburg
Mrs Bernard L Schwartz
Mrs Lisa Schwartz
Mrs D Scott
Mr and Mrs Richard Seymour
Mr Mark Shelmerdine
Mr R J Simmons CBE
Mr John H M Sims
Miss L M Slattery
Dr and Mrs M L Slotover
Mrs P Spanoghe
Professor Philip Stott
Mr James Stuart
Mr J A Tackaberry
Mr G C A Thorn
Mrs Andrew Trollope
Mr and Mrs Vignoles
Mrs Catherine I Vlasto
Mr and Mrs Ludovic de Walden
Miss J Waterous
Mrs Claire Weldon
Mr Frank S Wenstrom
Mrs Ann S Wilberding
Mr David Wilson
Mr W M Wood
Mr R M Woodhouse
Ms Karen S Yamada
Dr Alain Youell
Mrs Pia Zombanakis
*and others who wish to remain
anonymous*

CORPORATE MEMBERSHIP OF THE ROYAL ACADEMY

Launched in 1988, the Royal Academy's Corporate Membership Scheme has proved highly successful. With 115 members it is now the largest membership scheme in Europe. Corporate membership offers company benefits to staff and clients and access to the Academy's facilities and resources. Each member pays an annual subscription to be a Member (£6,000) or Patron (£20,000). Participating companies recognise the importance of promoting the visual arts. Their support is vital to the continuing success of the Academy.

CORPORATE MEMBERSHIP SCHEME

CORPORATE PATRONS
Arthur Andersen
Bloomberg LP
BP AMOCO plc
Debenhams Retail plc
The Economist Group
GE Group
Glaxo Wellcome plc
Merrill Lynch Mercury

Morgan Stanley International
Rover Group Limited

HONORARY CORPORATE PATRONS
Ernst & Young

CORPORATE MEMBERS
Alliance & Leicester plc
Apax Partners & Co. Ltd
Athenaeum Hotel
Aukett Associates
AXA Sun Life plc
Bacon and Woodrow
Bank of America
Bankers Trust
Banque Nationale de Paris
Barclays plc
Bear, Stearns International Ltd
BG plc
BICC plc
BMP DDB Limited
Bovis Europe
BT plc
British Airways Plc
British Alcan Aluminium plc
British American Tobacco plc
The Brunswick Group
Bunzl plc
CB Hillier Parker
CJA (Management Recruitment
   Consultants) Limited
Christie's
Chase Manhattan Bank
Chubb Insurance Company of Europe
Clayton Dubilier and Rice Limited
Clifford Chance
Colefax and Fowler Group
Cookson Group plc
Credit Agricole Indosuez
Credit Suisse First Boston
The Daily Telegraph plc
Deutsche Bank AG
Diageo plc
De Beers
E D & F Man Limited Charitable Trust
Eversheds
Foreign & Colonial Management plc
Gartmore Investment Management plc
Granada Group PLC
GTS Business Services
HSBC plc
Hay Management Consultants
Limited
H J Heinz Company Limited
ICI
John Lewis Partnership
King Sturge and Co.
Kleinwort Benson Charitable Trust
Korn/Ferry International
KPMG
Kvaerner Construction Ltd
Land Securities PLC
Lex Service PLC
Linklaters & Paines
Marks & Spencer
Marsh Ltd
McKinsey & Co.
Mitchell Madison Group
MoMart Ltd
Newton Investment Management Ltd
Ove Arup Partnership
Paribas
Pearson plc
The Peninsular and Oriental Steam
   Navigation Company

Pentland Group plc
PricewaterhouseCoopers
Provident Financial plc
The Rank Group PLC
Robert Fleming & Co. Ltd
Rothmans UK Holdings Limited
The Royal Bank of Scotland
Sainsbury's PLC
Salomon Smith Barney
Schroders plc
Sea Containers Ltd
SG
Slaughter and May
SmithKline Beecham
The Smith & Williamson Group
Sotheby's
Sun Life and Provincial Holdings plc
TI Group plc
Trowers & Hamlins
Unilever UK Limited
United Airlines
Wilde Sapte

HONORARY CORPORATE MEMBERS
All Nippon Airways Co. Ltd
A. T. Kearney Limited
Goldman Sachs International Limited
London First
Old Mutual
Reuters Limited
Yakult UK Limited

CORPORATE ASSOCIATES
Bass PLC
The General Electric Company plc
Macfarlanes
Save & Prosper Foundation

SPONSORS OF PAST EXHIBITIONS

The President and Council of the Royal Academy thank sponsors of past exhibitions for their support. Sponsors of major exhibitions during the last ten years have included the following:

Alitalia
Italian Art in the 20th Century, 1989
Allied Trust Bank
Africa: The Art of a Continent, 1995*
Anglo American Corporation of South Africa
Africa: The Art of a Continent, 1995*
A.T. Kearney
Summer Exhibition 99, 1999
Summer Exhibition 2000, 2000
The Banque Indosuez Group
Pissarro: The Impressionist and the City, 1993
Banque Indosuez and W. I. Carr
Gauguin and The School of Pont-Aven: Prints and Paintings, 1989
BBC Radio One
The Pop Art Show, 1991
BMW (GB) Limited
Georges Rouault: The Early Years, 1903–1920. 1993
David Hockney: A Drawing Retrospective, 1995*
British Airways Plc
Africa: The Art of a Continent, 1995
BT
Hokusai, 1991

Cantor Fitzgerald
From Manet to Gauguin: Masterpieces from Swiss Private Collections, 1995
The Capital Group Companies
Drawings from the J Paul Getty Museum, 1993
Chilstone Garden Ornaments
The Palladian Revival: Lord Burlington and His House and Garden at Chiswick, 1995
Christie's
Frederic Leighton 1830–1896, 1996
Sensation: Young British Artists from The Saatchi Collection, 1997
Classic FM
Goya: Truth and Fantasy, The Small Paintings, 1994
The Glory of Venice: Art in the Eighteenth Century, 1994
Corporation of London
Living Bridges, 1996
The Dai-Ichi Kangyo Bank Limited
222nd Summer Exhibition, 1990
The Daily Telegraph
American Art in the 20th Century, 1993
De Beers
Africa: The Art of a Continent, 1995
Debenhams Retail plc
Premiums, 2000
Final Year Show, 2000
Premiums, 2001
Deutsche Morgan Grenfell
Africa: The Art of a Continent, 1995
Diageo plc
230th Summer Exhibition, 1998
Digital Equipment Corporation
Monet in the '90s: The Series Paintings, 1990
The Drue Heinz Trust
The Palladian Revival: Lord Burlington and His House and Garden at Chiswick, 1995
Denys Lasdun, 1997
Tadao Ando: Master of Minimalism, 1998
The Dupont Company
American Art in the 20th Century, 1993
The Economist
Inigo Jones Architect, 1989
Edwardian Hotels
The Edwardians and After: Paintings and Sculpture from the Royal Academy's Collection, 1900–1950. 1990
Elf
Alfred Sisley, 1992
Ernst & Young
Monet in the 20th Century, 1999
Fiat
Italian Art in the 20th Century, 1989
Financial Times
Inigo Jones Architect, 1989
Flemings
Scottish Colourists, 2000
Fondation Elf
Alfred Sisley, 1992
Ford Motor Company Limited
The Fauve Landscape: Matisse, Derain, Braque and Their Circle, 1991
Friends of the Royal Academy
Victorian Fairy Painting, 1997
Gamlestaden
Royal Treasures of Sweden, 1550–1700. 1989

The Jacqueline and Michael Gee Charitable Trust
LIFE? or THEATRE? The Work of Charlotte Salomon, 1999
Générale des Eaux Group
Living Bridges, 1996
Glaxo Wellcome plc
Great Impressionist and other Master Paintings from the Emil G Buhrle Collection, Zurich, 1991
The Unknown Modigliani, 1994
Goldman Sachs International
Alberto Giacometti, 1901–1966, 1996
Picasso: Painter and Sculptor in Clay, 1998
The Guardian
The Unknown Modigliani, 1994
Guinness PLC (see Diageo plc)
Twentieth-Century Modern Masters: The Jacques and Natasha Gelman Collection, 1990
223rd Summer Exhibition, 1991
224th Summer Exhibition, 1992
225th Summer Exhibition, 1993
226th Summer Exhibition, 1994
227th Summer Exhibition, 1995
228th Summer Exhibition, 1996
229th Summer Exhibition, 1997
Guinness Peat Aviation
Alexander Calder, 1992
Harpers & Queen
Georges Rouault: The Early Years, 1903–1920. 1993
Sandra Blow, 1994
David Hockney: A Drawing Retrospective, 1995 ⚹
Roger de Grey, 1996
The Headley Trust
Denys Lasdun, 1997
The Henry Moore Foundation
Alexander Calder, 1992
Africa: The Art of a Continent, 1995
Ibstock Building Products Ltd
John Soane: Architect, Master of Space and Light, 1999
The Independent
The Art of Photography 1839–1989. 1989
The Pop Art Show, 1991
Living Bridges, 1996
Industrial Bank of Japan, Limited
Hokusai, 1991
Intercraft Designs Limited
Inigo Jones Architect, 1989
Donald and Jeanne Kahn
John Hoyland, 1999
The Kleinwort Benson Group
Inigo Jones Architect, 1989
Land Securities PLC
Denys Lasdun, 1997
Logica
The Art of Photography, 1839–1989. 1989
The Mail on Sunday
Royal Academy Summer Season, 1992
Royal Academy Summer Season, 1993
Marks & Spencer
Royal Academy Schools Premiums, 1994
Royal Academy Schools Final Year Show, 1994 ⚹
Martini & Rossi Ltd
The Great Age of British Watercolours, 1750–1880. 1993
Paul Mellon KBE
The Great Age of British Watercolours, 1750–1880 1993

Mercury Communications
The Pop Art Show, 1991
Merrill Lynch
American Art in the 20th Century, 1993 ⚹
Midland Bank plc
The Art of Photography 1839–1989. 1989
RA Outreach Programme, 1992–1996
Lessons in Life, 1994
Minorco
Africa: The Art of a Continent, 1995
Mitsubishi Estate Company UK Limited
Sir Christopher Wren and the Making of St Paul's, 1991
Natwest Group
Nicolas Poussin 1594–1665. 1995
The Nippon Foundation
Hiroshige: Images of Mist, Rain, Moon and Snow, 1997
Olivetti
Andrea Mantegna, 1992
Park Tower Realty Corporation
Sir Christopher Wren and the Making of St Paul's, 1991
Peterborough United Football Club
Art Treasures of England: The Regional Collections, 1997
Premiercare (National Westminster Insurance Services)
Roger de Grey, 1996 ⚹
RA Exhibition Patrons Group
Chagall: Love and the Stage, 1998
Kandinsky, 1999
Chardin 1699–1779, 2000
Redab (UK) Ltd
Wisdom and Compassion: The Sacred Art of Tibet, 1992
Reed Elsevier plc
Van Dyck 1599–1641, 1999
Reed International plc
Sir Christopher Wren and the Making of St Paul's, 1991
Republic National Bank of New York
Sickert: Paintings, 1992
The Royal Bank of Scotland
Braque: The Late Works, 1997 ⚹
Premiums, 1997
Premiums, 1998
Premiums, 1999
Royal Academy Schools Final Year Show, 1996
Royal Academy Schools Final Year Show, 1997
Royal Academy Schools Final Year Show, 1998
The Sara Lee Foundation
Odilon Redon: Dreams and Visions, 1995
Sea Containers Ltd
The Glory of Venice: Art in the Eighteenth Century, 1994
Silhouette Eyewear
Egon Schiele and His Contemporaries: From the Leopold Collection, Vienna, 1990
Wisdom and Compassion: The Sacred Art of Tibet, 1992
Sandra Blow, 1994
Africa: The Art of a Continent, 1995
Société Générale, UK
Gustave Caillebotte: The Unknown Impressionist, 1996 ⚹

Société Générale de Belgique
Impressionism to Symbolism: The Belgian Avant-Garde 1880–1900. 1994
Spero Communications
Royal Academy Schools Final Year Show, 1992
Texaco
Selections from the Royal Academy's Private Collection, 1991
Thames Water Plc
Thames Water Habitable Bridge Competition, 1996
The Times
Wisdom and Compassion: The Sacred Art of Tibet, 1992
Drawings from the J Paul Getty Museum, 1993
Goya: Truth and Fantasy, The Small Paintings, 1994
Africa: The Art of a Continent, 1995
Time Out
Sensation: Young British Artists from The Saatchi Collection, 1997
Tractabel
Impressionism to Symbolism: The Belgian Avant-Garde 1880–1900. 1994
Unilever
Frans Hals, 1990
Union Minière
Impressionism to Symbolism: The Belgian Avant-Garde 1880–1900. 1994
Vistech International Ltd
Wisdom and Compassion: The Sacred Art of Tibet, 1992
Yakult UK Ltd
RA Outreach Programme, 1997–2000 ⚹

⚹ Recipients of a Pairing Scheme Award, managed by Arts + Business. Arts + Business is funded by the Arts Council of England and the Department for Culture, Media and Sport

OTHER SPONSORS

Sponsors of events, publications and other items in the past two years:

Atlantic Group plc
Elizabeth Blackadder RA
BP AMOCO p.l.c.
Country Life
Foster and Partners
Green's Restaurant
IBJ International plc
John Doyle Construction
Allen Jones RA
Michael Hopkins & Partners
Morgan Stanley Dean Witter
Old Mutual
Richard and Ruth Rogers
Strutt & Parker